STORIES

FROM

55

BROAD STREET

September 11, 2001

Barry,
Take time for
the things that
matter. Mary Sillus

To Barry, may you share
in our memories.
Heidi Murphy
p. 83

STORIES

FROM

55

BROAD STREET

To Barry —
Colleague and friend.
All good wishes
Ray Roland

September 11, 2001
Lower Manhattan
New York, New York

Library of Congress Preassigned Control Number: 2002102822
Jones, David A.
         Stories from 55 Broad Street
         Photographs by Anthony Choate and Diane Davis
         ISBN 0-9718042-1-4

Cover design: Miriam Hansen
Composition by Allentown Digital Services Division of RR Donnelley & Sons

Published by
DAJ Publishing, LLC
P.O. Box 549
Louisville, Kentucky 40201-0549

www.StoriesFrom55Broad.com

INTRODUCTION

The destruction of the World Trade Center and the deaths of thousands of our fellow citizens have indelibly marked every American. For those in New York's financial district on September 11, 2001, the proximity of the violence produced a unique set of impressions. Twenty-three Humana employees, gathered at 55 Broad Street to launch a new digital health plan, were among them. In hopes that their experiences will help us all come to terms with the meaning and consequences of that horrific day—to hearten the living, even as we honor the dead—these stories are set forth.

I would like to extend my thanks to each contributor. It is not an easy task to record one's thoughts and emotions about events so traumatic, so personal and so recently past. I was proud to count myself among you on the 11th in New York. Today I am prouder still.

My special thanks as well to Diane Davis and Anthony Choate, whose dramatic photographs form an indispensable portion of this account. I'm also grateful to Diane for coordinating the production of this book with sensitivity and decision, and to Tom Noland, our inspired editor. Finally, all of us at 55 Broad Street on September 11 are indebted to our fellow Humana associates, who gave us such unstinting support, help and encouragement, that day and after.

David A. Jones
Chairman of the Board
Humana Inc.

TABLE OF CONTENTS

ACKNOWLEDGMENTS

The Humana associates whose stories appear in this book would like to acknowledge the following people and companies for their kind assistance:

Crystal Tours, Inc. and Adam

Digital Sandbox staff

Eat 'N Park, Harrisburg, Pa.

Farrell's Car Service, New York

SEPTEMBER 11 MEMORIES

Beth Bierbower

The events of September 11th are well documented. We have seen the tragedy through the eyes of an objective camera and the voices of the survivors or the loved ones of those who lost—or gave—their lives to save others. But each of us, whether we watched the events unfold on television or were close enough to witness the devastation, have indelible memories and we are changed forever.

I will forever remember. . . .

- The last beautiful glimpse of the New York City skyline from the Windows on the World restaurant the evening before the tragedy.
- The deli in the WTC complex that I visited at 6:00 A.M. the morning of September 11 for breakfast. Is the man that helped me all right? Is he alive?
- The thunderous sound as the second plane crashed and the shock and devastation on the faces of my co-workers who were witnesses to that event.
- The supportive hug from my friend and co-worker as I waited to learn more about the plane crash near Pittsburgh, my home, and ensure that my family was safe.
- The September 11th e-mail that I read one day later from my son. It was short. It was frantic. I can only imagine the fear that my family felt, knowing I was in the vicinity but not knowing whether I was safe.
- Walking through the deserted streets of Manhattan during the middle of the afternoon and feeling as if I was in another world.
- Watching from a hotel room in Times Square as the third building in the WTC complex twisted and crumbled—more destruction, more devastation.
- Arriving in Pittsburgh over a day later and learning that two high school classmates were on the flights that crashed into the towers. One classmate was a longtime friend.

As I share these memories I know that the reality is that I am alive and surrounded by loved ones. For this I am grateful beyond words. Many individuals are not so fortunate. Their memories are painful and they live day in and day out with a bitter reality that they will never see their loved ones again. We should remember and honor these individuals by continuing to make America the greatest country on this earth, a country that symbolizes strength, unity and above all, freedom.

AFTER THE SMOKE

Dick Brown

After the smoke, debris and chaos of 9-11-01, I have wondered why: why some and not others? Why innocent children on board out-of-control airplanes? Why some escaped seemingly insurmountable odds and escaped the collapsed buildings, yet others who had opportunities to flee the buildings, stayed behind to help others? Or, as in one case, stayed behind to be with a wheelchair-bound quadriplegic friend who knew he would never make it out alive?

Reason has no place in this story. The senseless acts of a few have destroyed the lives of thousands, if not millions. The impact is not brief, it is eternal. I cannot reason why we decided to leave the Marriott World Trade Center at 8:40 instead of 8:45 as we had once planned. I cannot reason why we were able to get away from the area without incident. Nor can I reason why two dozen Humana executives, wandering along the streets of Lower Manhattan, came upon a bus that would eventually be our means of Exodus from New York.

For those of us who believe in the power of prayer, it is perhaps a comfort. It is a natural and spiritual cloak on which we cling, clinging to hope and confidence that we will be delivered. That was my prayer as we trudged along the gray, silent streets seeking shelter for the night. That the prayer was answered is not a surprise. That it was answered so quickly should not have been, but was. I really did not get the full effect of that until later, as we were bouncing along the Jersey Turnpike heading for Harrisburg, Pennsylvania.

My questions about why, and why not? Well, I still do not know those answers. Perhaps it is not up to me to try and determine why some perish while others walk away. I do know this—I have been given another day, another week, another month and, perhaps, another year. We all have. It should be our goal or calling if you will, to make sure each of those days counts for something or someone. My desire each day is to do something good for at least one person before I rest. To do less would make my walk away from New York meaningless.

The World Trade Center towers moments before the second plane hit.

MY MEMORIES: THE EVENTS OF SEPTEMBER 11, 2001

Luisa Charbonneau

On September 10th we arrived in New York. We were in the midst of final preparations for the unveiling of the Emphesys product. After so many months of designing and building a great new product, we were getting the chance to show it off to the media and selected guests. The event, scheduled for the next morning, promised to be a great success. It was going to be held at the "Digital Sandbox," a high-tech venue in New York City. After the final rehearsals, several members of the senior staff were hosting dinners for key vendors and clients. Because of its vicinity and the flexibility it offered, I had suggested we hold the dinners at Windows on the World at the top of the Trade Center. Eileen Hutchison made all of the arrangements. Several of us who were not involved in the planned dinners went off to another restaurant for dinner but considered having a drink at the top of the World Trade Center to take in the view. It was a dismal rainy evening so we decided to forgo the two-block walk, and headed back to our hotel, the Marriott Financial Center.

The next morning we gathered in the hotel lobby waiting for the limousine service to arrive with two vans to take us to 55 Broad Street for the event. The vans were scheduled to arrive at 8:30 but they were running late. I looked at my watch; it was 8:40. I stepped outside to use my cell phone to call and check on them. It was a beautiful crisp clear morning. The dispatchers from Farrell's were trying to contact their van drivers by radio—I was getting nervous thinking, "The guests should be arriving at 9:00 . . . where are those vans?" Finally I got a reply. They said the first van was only two blocks away and a second van was ten minutes away. I went back to the lobby to let the group know. We gathered our suitcases and headed to the curb. It was a pretty large van; if we squeezed in, we could all fit and not risk being late to the event. The van driver headed toward the Digital Sandbox. He was going to pick us up after the event so he was insistent that we leave our luggage with him; after all, why would we want to lug suitcases with us? We realized that we weren't all leaving together and it would just be simpler if we took our suitcases with us. Diane Davis was sure there was a room available where we could store them until the event was over. The bus got quiet, we were just looking out of the windows at the traffic, and blue sky. Suddenly I heard Ken Fasola say, "The top of the World Trade Center just exploded." I turned to look over my left shoulder at him and saw him staring out of the window. I said "No way, that can't be." I kept thinking surely he's mistaken. We all stared in disbelief. Above us only a couple of blocks away was a large cloud of smoke, flames and . . . ticker tape?!! I kept staring at the tiny pieces of paper just hanging in the sky. Only I realized, they weren't just pieces of paper, they were shimmering, they were millions of pieces of glass. They seemed to float in the air in slow motion.

Our driver was looking out of the side window, continuing to drive straight ahead, and exclaiming how he had "been here the first time the World Trade Center was bombed."

It just wasn't sinking in. What could have happened? I didn't comprehend the magnitude of the disaster that was beginning to unfold. We arrived at the Digital Sandbox a few minutes later, still ready to get on with the event. By now bits of charred paper and debris were starting to fall to the sidewalk. As we entered the building I saw most of my colleagues gathered around a television set next to the security desk. Stunned, they stared into the TV. People saying, "a plane flew into the World Trade Center." All I could think was, "How could any pilot not avoid the World Trade Center?" Even with 16 years of military service under my belt, it never occurred to me that this was anything but a horrible accident.

Some of our group went upstairs; others stayed in the lobby. I stepped outside to get a closer look at what was happening. As I advanced onto the sidewalk I heard a horrendous explosion. People started to run down the street and sidewalk toward me. Following close behind them was more debris and a cloud of smoke. People starting to yell—"another one hit."

We gathered our suitcases and briefcases and headed up to the fourth floor. Televisions were on upstairs so we could watch from relative safety as the events continued to progress. It was surreal. There is no other way to describe it. I felt numb, and couldn't fathom that what I was seeing with my own eyes was real. We needed to start making calls, cancel the event. We knew that our families, friends and colleagues at home would be worried. Everyone was trying fruitlessly to call home on cell phones. None worked. We finally found a couple of pay phones. I knew my husband was in Florida in an aircraft simulator for training and probably hadn't heard yet. On the other hand, my parents would be frantic, so I called them first to tell them I was OK. They had just returned from dropping off my children at school, so they hadn't seen the television yet. Next I called my husband. I got his cell phone and left him a message. He later told me how eerily calm I sounded on the voice mail. I said, "You will probably hear about this soon, I just want you to know I'm OK, we are all safe. I'll call you when I can." I didn't even think about the kids in school, but fortunately Marsden Kucera did, and we headed back to the pay phones. Marsden called her administrative assistant, who agreed to call our children's schools to let them know we were all right.

We waited and watched together. A solid team, supporting each other. All a little scared, but all mostly in shock. Everyone reacted a little differently outwardly. On the inside I think each of us felt confused, and dazed. I almost felt guilty for being calm and safe, and for not being able to do anything to help.

There was plenty of food; we were ready for a catered event for 150 people. I couldn't touch a bite. The building team tried to bring as many of the people into the building to the fourth floor. At least the food was put to good use. At one point I did gather a few of the bottles of juice and water that had been stashed under a table. I thought we better keep them for later. I wasn't sure how long we would have to stay there, and I wasn't sure if the water lines wouldn't become contaminated before long. That is if the air handler system didn't give out first. The sounds of sirens from emergency response vehicles came from all directions.

When the first tower collapsed, I felt heartsick and yet it still seemed like a bad dream. I looked out of the window. It was as dark as midnight. I put my hand up to one of the windows; it was warm to the touch.

I watched in horror at the television pictures from the Pentagon, thinking of the dozens, if not hundreds of friends and colleagues I know who work there. Fearful for each of them, and feeling absolutely powerless to help, here or there. I guess it was only a matter of time before the terrorists hit us on our own turf. It is so much easier to think that these kinds of things only happen to someone else, somewhere else.

The time all seems to run together now. At some point in the morning, the building management suggested that we go to the basement. Perhaps they were fearful of bombs, subsequent attacks or simply the possible damage from debris. Most of our group headed to the basement. I did not. I was sure I was safer on the fourth floor than in the basement. The last thing I wanted was to be trapped under rubble in a basement. The air quality was fine on the fourth floor; I wasn't sure what to expect in the basement.

Once the smoke began to clear and sunlight made its way through the smoke I noticed the cars were covered with a couple of inches of "gray snow." There was almost no one outside.

The building staff was wonderful. They were calm and organized. They were vigilant in their security—calling people to the lobby to greet visitors searching for friends or family, rather than letting unknown people wander through the building. They made copies of area maps so people could plan escape routes. They arranged for physicians to be on stand-by in the lobby if needed. They kept us informed. I can't say enough about the great job they did in handling the people inside their building.

The local news started to report gas leaks in the area. We knew we had to leave. But we had to have a plan first. If we left the building, we were unlikely to get back in. Some people were on the phone trying to find hotel rooms, others trying to find rental cars. Whatever we did, we had to stick together. I'm grateful that Mr. Jones and others who were familiar with the area came up with some options. They came up with a plan. If we walked Uptown, one of the Humana associates had a daughter with an apartment. Several of us could stay there. Mr. Jones had an apartment a little farther north. We'd stop at the first apartment and whoever could continue on would go to the second apartment. We would figure out a way home from there.

We all worked together. One group was tearing up tablecloths so we could wear them as masks to filter out the smoke. Others rounded up members of the group. Communicate the plan, find a buddy and stick with him or her—taking roll, so we left no one behind. We gathered in the lobby. Checking off each person as they emerged from the elevators, and taking a final roll call before we left the building. Our associates from the PR and production agencies were headed to different destinations and opted to stay behind. I still hated to leave them.

We left by way of the back door, Bruce Goodman on point, dragging our luggage behind us. A thick layer of ash covered everything; tiny bits of paper lying next to whole undamaged sheets of paper were scattered everywhere. A Microsoft Project timeline lay neatly in the middle of the sidewalk. The streets were deserted. It was a war zone. Unnerving at best. The smell of smoke filled the air.

Fortunately, we didn't have to walk that far. After about 20 minutes or so we happened upon a bus. I'm convinced we had a guardian angel with us. With so many people fleeing the area, to find an empty bus, just the right size, and a driver willing to take the group was nothing short of a miracle. Bruce and others did a great job of negotiating. We dropped off Beth Bierbower in Times Square. Her husband, an executive with a department store in Pittsburgh, arranged for a bus from Pittsburgh to pick up Beth and several of his employees and take them back to Pittsburgh. We dropped off two more people in town and headed toward New Jersey. The driver agreed to take us all the way to Harrisburg, Pa. Trouble hadn't left us just yet however; somewhere in New Jersey we blew a tire. More adventure as we looked for a tire to fit the tour bus, and then to find diesel fuel. Finally, the first food all day—popcorn, Cheez-its and a soda from the vending machines at a golf driving range in New Jersey. I have to say they tasted pretty darn good at that point.

The bus ride was long, but the company was pleasant. We had a chance to get to know each other a little better. We pulled into Harrisburg, Pa. at about 9:00 P.M. I've never been so happy to see a Trailways bus. We were all ready for dinner. We tried several restaurants but most had already closed their kitchens, though a nice cold beer was found at one stop. By the time we pulled into the "Eat 'N Park" we were all starving. Hamburgers, fries and chocolate milkshakes seemed to be the order of the day. The staff was so nice, one waitress made a point to come over and tell us she was keeping us in her prayers for a safe trip home. Another gave us a bag of cookies to go.

Exhaustion and a full stomach—it didn't take long to fall asleep. It was a fitful sleep, waking every hour or so. In the middle of the night I woke up, looked around, everyone was asleep, and I finally started to cry. I really wanted to sob, but I felt as if I had to pull myself together. Besides, I didn't even have a Kleenex.

It was almost harder to read about it in the paper the next morning when we stopped at McDonald's for breakfast outside Cincinnati, than it had been being there. It was a pretty quiet breakfast. We were all tired, mentally and physically, and anxious to get home.

It's somewhat odd, almost all of us went home briefly, showered, changed and came into work at least for a short time. I guess it was a longing for normalcy. Thankfully, all of us and all of our colleagues made it home safe and sound. There were several people I thought about over the last couple of weeks, and hoped they were safe. There was the lady who appeared in the Digital Sandbox with a 3-year-old little girl. She was dropping her off at school, when everything started to happen. She didn't want to leave her there, so she took the little girl with her. Unfortunately, she had no way to contact the child's mother to let her know that her daughter was safe. Then there were the van drivers that headed back to the hotel to pick up the luggage that some of our group left at the hotel. I finally called Susan at the Digital Sandbox, who stayed in the building until everyone left. She reported that the lady made contact with the child's mother and they planned a rendezvous point and a way home. The limousine service reports that all of the drivers are safe and accounted for.

THE
WORLD
CHANGES

Anthony Choate

Tuesday, September 11 dawned bright and beautiful over New York City, a day filled with promise and excitement. The sun coming up over the harbor cast a long shadow from the Statue of Liberty, making her appear larger than life. In downtown Manhattan, the street-level canyons were bathed in deep shadows while the twin towers of the World Trade Center rose high above it all, glistening in the sunlight.

The city was already amidst its usual hustle and bustle as we waited outside the Marriott Financial Center Hotel for our van to arrive. We were bound for the Global Communities Digital Sandbox just five blocks away at 55 Broad Street, one short block from the New York Stock Exchange. Half of our team was staying in the Marriott Financial Center Hotel while the other half was in the Marriott World Trade Center Hotel less than a block away.

New York radiates energy. You can't help but be charged just by standing in a crowd and gazing at the skyline. It's that kind of place.

And this is not simply the first impression of a hillbilly coming to the big city. I have visited New York City many times. I have relatives who have lived there for years. The more I visit, the more it grows on me. I can remember the first time that Maureen (my wife) visited her sister in the city. Her first comment after returning home was "Sell the house! We're moving!" Most days I can totally agree with that sentiment.

I had been in town since late Sunday night with a crew of other Humana associates. We were preparing for the presentation of our Emphesys Internet product launch to the media and financial communities. We had spent a long day on Monday getting the displays, systems, staging, lights, projection screens and live Web feeds ready for the big event.

Somewhere around 5 P.M. the stream of Humana executives began to arrive for the final rehearsals. Our Hollywood producer had created a video backdrop reminiscent of Apple's "Tearing Down the Walls" campaign, which grabbed media and public attention a few years ago. He wanted this presentation to be perfect and proceeded to march Mike McCallister, Jack Lord and Bruce Goodman through repeated rehearsals. Once was not enough. Twice was not enough. As is often said, the third time was a charm. But this was not a short presentation. When you complete a full rehearsal three times you have an evening that would make "War and Peace" seem short.

Finally, all adjustments had been made. Hunger was taking over. It was time for some food and a stroll around town. Mike, Jack, and Bruce were hosting dinner for about thirty invitees at the Windows on the World restaurant atop the World Trade Center. It was a gorgeous night for taking in the intoxicating view of the city that never sleeps. From the restaurant, you can gaze far below and marvel at the imagination, creativity, talent and skills that were amassed to create the World Trade Center.

Nine people from our group went to the China Grill on 53rd Street where Mary Sellers proceeded to order appetizers and dinner for everyone at the table. This is a place where every order is made to be shared and every diner at the table was able to sample an exotic array of food. Though everyone had their fill, we had two small bags left over to take back with us as we grudgingly left.

Sam Garas and I were familiar with the city so we led a short walking tour. We took some of our co-workers to Rockefeller Center, a couple of the TV studios and Times Square. The bright lights of the big city never fail to impress. We ended the tour with a subway ride downtown. We got off at the World Trade Center stop and wandered through the maze of shops beneath the building. It was a very promising evening as everyone headed back to his or her room for the night.

Tuesday morning began early with TV interviews at the American Stock Exchange for Mike and Tom Noland. Others had scattered to various restaurants and coffee shops to grab some breakfast before heading to 55 Broad Street. The non-breakfast crowd was checking out of the Marriott Financial Center Hotel and waiting for transportation.

At 8:40 A.M. our van arrived and we started loading up for the short ride to the Digital Sandbox. Even on a bad day, it would only have been about a 15-minute walk. Gene Shields, Ken Fasola, Eileen Hutchison, Diane Davis, Denise Damron, Marcia Jaggers, Sam, Luisa Charbonneau, and I packed ourselves in and, amid laughter and excitement, we were off.

We pulled into the busy traffic, merged across three lanes with the obligatory honking of horns, and made a U-turn directly in front of the Marriott World Trade Center Hotel. We glanced over at the sidewalk to see if there were any other Humana associates waiting for a ride and looked out the rear window at the twin towers.

We had driven two blocks when we all heard a loud explosion. Ken shouted, "Oh my God, the Trade Center just blew up!" All bodies immediately leaned to the left side of the van. Faces and hands pressed against the windows, trying to look up high enough to see what was happening.

A bright orange ball of flame engulfed the upper portion of one of the towers and a large plume of black smoke was already rising to fill the sky. Millions of pieces of paper began a slow-motion descent toward the streets below. As we watched, we could see shattered pieces of glass glittering in the sunshine. They looked like tiny mirrors rushing past the pieces of paper in a surreal race to be the first to reach the ground.

Diane had a digital camera and began to shoot a few photos as we instructed our driver to get us to the Digital Sandbox quickly. Within minutes the streets would be closed to all traffic as fire trucks, ambulances, and other emergency vehicles sped to the disaster site. People were running from the area at the base of the tower in an attempt to avoid the falling debris. Onlookers were staring upward, hands over mouths, shocked looks on their faces.

We assumed that a bomb had been detonated in the tower, but no one could believe that a bomb sizable enough to cause that much destruction could have been moved into the building without being noticed. We watched with the realization that many hundreds of people were dying at that very moment. Our driver pressed on in an effort to get us to our location.

Upon arriving at 55 Broad Street, we decided to take our luggage into the building with us, thinking our van driver might not be able to make it back later. As we proceeded into the lobby, a huge crowd of people was gathered watching a wall of TVs that had originally been programmed to display a demonstration of Humana's Emphesys product launch. This wall contained a grid of six horizontally placed TVs and six vertically placed TVs—36 in total. Each could display a separate image or the images could be combined into groups of four or more. The pictures on all 36 TVs were now combined to display a wall-sized image of the gaping hole in the side of the World Trade Center.

Across the bottom of the screens, a scrolling banner repeated the message, "A 767 commercial jet has crashed into the World Trade Center." How could an accident of this magnitude happen? Airplanes have crashed before but I had only heard of a single incident of one hitting a building, and that was a small military jet that crashed into a hotel in Indianapolis many years ago. As we waited for additional details, the image of another jet plane came swooping out of the sky in a large curving arc straight toward the second tower. This one hit the tower at a lower level than the first and looked like it would slice the building into two separate pieces. My first thought was that the upper section of the tower would topple over into the street below.

Everyone realized that this was an intentional and premeditated attack. Our hearts were in our throats as we thought of all of the people on the two planes and in both towers who were immediately killed. I kept hoping that there had been enough time after the first explosion for people to evacuate. But I was also afraid that many probably stayed in their offices, never imagining that their lives were in danger. Sirens were the only sound. No cars, no honking horns, no loud New York pedestrian traffic. All of that was gone, only sirens. There were reports that some people had chosen to leap from the building rather than face the raging fire that rapidly approached them. I could not watch.

At that point, building security urged everyone to go to the basement or stay on the lower floors until it could be determined if additional attacks were coming. We were instructed to stay away from the large glass lobby area to avoid shattering glass. There was serious concern that the New York Stock Exchange, which was a block away, could be a target. People were already fleeing the Exchange building. They were easily recognizable in their colored trading jackets. Our group made its way to the fourth floor of 55 Broad Street and started considering our options.

An unexpected addition to the group was Humana's founder David Jones. He had just returned from vacation on Monday and had decided to fly to New York on Tuesday morning to be a part of the Emphesys presentation. He had been sitting in the Starbucks coffee shop next to the 55 Broad Street building when the first tower was hit. He immediately came next door where he found many of the Humana associates already gathered.

The management team found a room where they could begin the ordeal of contacting the corporate office and making decisions about what to do. The mood was somber as people attempted to contact family and friends to let them know we were safe. That feeling lasted only a brief moment as the large screen projection system displayed the video feed of the collapse of one of the twin towers. One of the tallest buildings in the world was crumbling to the ground right before our eyes. We could look out the windows and see it going down. Hundreds of firemen and rescue workers had entered the building to try to reach the trapped and injured. We watched as a dark cloud of dust, ash, and the souls of its occupants rushed toward us. It was the color of disease. It was a sickly, dirty brown maelstrom created from the incineration and collapse that enveloped us and turned a crystal clear day to total blackness.

The smell of smoke filled the air. The anxiety level increased and was displayed on the faces of everyone. People became much more nervous and unsure of their safety. Leaving the building was now no longer an option. We cut up T-shirts and tablecloths to use as face masks in case the smoke got thicker. Luckily, the building's mechanical system recirculated the inside air rather that pulling in air from outside. Occasionally, you would see some tears as people realized that this was now a vastly more dangerous situation than we had been in only moments before. The local authorities closed all bridges and tunnels into Manhattan except for those on the far northern end of town. The subways were shut off and city buses were used to block all streets at Midtown. We were now in an isolated disaster zone. No one would be allowed into the area. The reporters had labeled it "Ground Zero," a reference commonly used to designate the site of a nuclear explosion.

Our cell phones were unusable. All circuits were overloaded and no calls were making it in or out. Jason Largever, vice president of the New York Information Technology Center and his crew quickly removed the long-distance dialing restriction from their phone system and plugged in additional phones. People struggled to contact anyone outside of New York who might be able to relay a message for them. In the rare event that someone actually got a call through to a family member, their façade of strength quickly faded into relieved tears and an unsteady voice as they spoke of the situation.

We had already taken a roll call and verified the presence of all but three members of our team. Calls were being made from all over in an effort to locate them. The first good news came when we heard that Art Hipwell had not been able to make his flight to New York that morning. We still did not know the whereabouts of Judi Farmer or Bob Walt. Judi would be arriving in New York by way of a Washington, D.C. stopover. She was supposed to be leaving from National. People were very worried. There were people in New York and Louisville attempting to determine her location. We finally got word that her flight had not left National Airport. A collective sigh of relief went through the room.

Where was Bob? He had left to have breakfast with a couple of our clients that morning and had not been heard from since. Long after we had located everyone else, we received word that Bob had been only two blocks from the tower when it collapsed. His group had been caught outside by the dust and smoke and were covered from head to toe. He had quickly pulled a T-shirt out of his suitcase to cover his face and crouched behind a wall to wait for some visibility to return. Eventually, he was able to make his way to Battery Park and catch a ferry to New Jersey where he located a rental car to drive to Louisville. Our spirits were a little lighter. All of our team members were accounted for.

The air was beginning to clear. We could see some people on the street trying to leave the area. It looked like a good time for us to think about leaving too. That's when the second tower crumbled into a smoldering heap. The sky went black again. The relaxed mood that was beginning to return was quickly erased. The tragedy kept getting worse with each minute. Our only thoughts were, "Please let people have gotten out before it fell."

The smell of smoke returned once more, along with the anxiety and feelings of helplessness. We watched the smoke and ash blow against the windows and settle on the ledges of our building. Often, you could not even see the ledge. The scene on the projection screens was even more depressing as we watched numerous buildings disappear within the expanding cloud. The enormity of the devastation was overwhelming. I cannot believe that even the crazed mind of a terrorist would ever envision such total destruction.

Leaving the building was still not an option. We were left watching the news coverage to learn what was happening around us while at the same time trying not to think about the increasing number of people who were dying just four blocks away. Would it be totally cold and callous to try to block the entire scene from your mind? Or would it be the only way to safeguard your sanity? Would it be a sign of weakness to shed tears for those suffering around us? We cried anyway.

People sat watching the large TV screens. People sat in small groups, conversing quietly. People stood by the windows, waiting to see the sky again. People continued to make phone contact with family, friends and associates. Some were successful. Others just kept trying. We had nowhere to go and no way to get there but we knew that we would have to leave at the first reasonably safe opportunity. We made facemasks for everyone by cutting up T-shirts and tablecloths and dipping them in water. We searched our bags and found pants for those who were wearing skirts and shoes that would be better for walking. We gathered our belongings and made sure that we knew where all of the members of our group were located. Then we waited some more.

As everyone struggled to remain patient and calm, there came the announcement that a third plane had crashed into the Pentagon in Washington, D.C., causing many more deaths. A fourth hijacked plane had crashed in rural Pennsylvania. There were no survivors. How many more could there possibly be? Of greater concern to us was whether there would be planes aimed at other buildings nearby.

Time passed slowly. The air outside began to clear. There continued to be enough dust and smoke to cause some degree of breathing difficulty and eye irritation for those who ventured outside. The news continued to bombard us with depressing views of destruction, death, grief, mourning and hope. There was always hope that at least one more person would be found alive in the wreckage.

The sun was still shining as the smoke thinned. Thousands of people worked furiously, digging through the intensely hot rubble—enduring cuts, scrapes, bruises, scratched and irritated eyes, and coughing fits caused by the smoke and dust—all because they kept a small spark of hope alive within them that someone inside was alive and waiting for rescue.

There comes a point when the scenes become too much and you have to completely remove them from your mind so that you can return to thinking and functioning in a normal fashion. You let go of the despair, turn away from the television and do not look back. You can change nothing that has happened, so you become determined to focus on the task of planning what to do next. That's what happened to me.

Two o'clock came and we decided that it is was time to leave. A police officer had suggested that when we leave the building, we should proceed east, toward the river and away from the hazardous areas, then turn north and head for Midtown. The thirty members of our group gathered in the elevator area of the first floor and took roll call. The building security guards told us that we are not allowed in this area. Someone told them sternly that we would leave the moment that everyone was accounted for. They finally let us finish our roll call.

We were not allowed to exit via the front doors, and were instead led through a maze of hallways and out a door that opened into an area by the loading dock. The smoke smell was strong and people pulled their scarves up over their mouths and noses. Our footsteps caused little clouds of dust to rise up and coat our shoes and clothing.

There was an unnatural quietness as we walked. There were other groups of people scattered about with surgical masks, cloth masks or jacket collars held across their faces. Everyone was slowly and somberly making their way toward Midtown Manhattan. We walked by a police van that had been hit by some flying object that had broken the windshield. It sat abandoned on the sidewalk.

All of the businesses were closed and dark. Occasionally you would see people standing inside the windows, watching the exodus. One small shop owner had already started to clean the area in front of his store. He had a hose and broom and was valiantly attempting a return to normalcy by removing the dust from his storefront and sidewalk and washing the windows.

As we walked north, the coating of dust became noticeably thinner. It was like the point in the movie "The Wizard of Oz" where the film changed from black and white to full color. Where everything behind had been covered with a dull gray layer of dust, the natural world of color had suddenly re-emerged around us. We were starting to see more people standing on street corners, all staring back toward downtown, watching the smoke billowing above what was left of the World Trade Center. The cloud rose a few hundred feet above the skyline, then took an abrupt horizontal turn toward the north and stretched all the way Uptown across the length of Manhattan.

We continued our trek northward. We had been unable to get any hotel accommodations in the city. Mr. Jones had an apartment somewhere around 69th Street. Sam had a sister living in Midtown. One of the Humana corporate jet pilots had family living in lower Midtown. A few would be able to meet other family members or relatives around the Times Square area. We had decided to place some members of our group in each of these locations until plans could be made to get everyone home.

We had only been walking 30 minutes when our own little miracle occurred. We happened upon a Crystal Tour bus parked along Madison Street. The operator had the hood up and was leaning over the engine checking out a problem, which appeared to be corrected. Mr. Jones, Mike, and Bruce approached him and began negotiations to convince him to take our group to the various drop-offs. The driver, a young Hispanic gentleman named Adam, seemed a little reluctant. He looked a little worried as the group of us huddled nearby. His mood changed to relief as the negotiations progressed, and soon we were loading our luggage into the rear compartment of the bus.

This was a small city tour bus that had 28 seats and large oversized windows. It was designed to allow people unrestricted viewing as they were being given a tour of New York City. We started loading our group of 30 onto the bus, doubling-up on a couple of seats to get everyone in. As we were boarding, an elderly lady approached our group asking if we could make room for one more rider to Midtown. Someone stood in the aisle and gave her a seat. Although we did not get her name, we did find out that she was a 1948 graduate of the University of Louisville Kent School of Social Work. It was a pretty strange coincidence to encounter another stranded Louisvillian in this city of millions.

Our moods brightened as we made our way northward. Negotiations were still going on near the front of the bus between Mike, Bruce, Ken, and Adam. They convinced Adam to drop off some people around Times Square and then take the rest to either New Jersey or Philadelphia to search for some rental cars.

Somewhere near lower Midtown, we were forced to take a left and head straight west. City buses had been placed on all north-south streets to block traffic access to the downtown area. All bridges, tunnels and subways had been shut down. The only means to exit the city was by proceeding to the west side of Manhattan and taking the river road north until it reached the George Washington Bridge. Traffic was crawling as we crossed the Midtown area. We made a couple of stops to let some people off then continued on.

The scene was like something out of a war movie. Thousands of refugees lining the road for miles and miles as they slowly make their way to the border. We took our place in this massive exodus and slowly progressed northward. Eventually, we reached the bridge and left Manhattan.

The pace of traffic picked up considerably as we made our way over the George Washington Bridge. The little bus increased its speed, but we soon found out that its suspension system was not designed for the open road. Every uneven transition in the pavement caused it to bottom out with a bone-jarring thud. It felt like the poor thing was scraping the road. The thuds stopped until we crossed the New Jersey State line. Then a sudden "bam," and a loud "whap, whap, whap" that sent a jolt through everyone. Luckily, it was only a blowout of one of the rear tires.

We pulled over and Adam got out to check out the condition of his bus. There were four tires on the rear of the bus and only one had blown out. The remaining tires looked sound enough to get us to the next exit. We located the nearest tire dealer and Adam went in to make arrangements to get the tire replaced. Unfortunately, they did not have a replacement for us, but another shop nearby did. Adam and Steve Moya took the bus to have the tire replaced.

Meanwhile, our group descended on a small golf driving range to get some drinks and snacks. Most of us had eaten little or nothing all day and were starting to get hungry. The process of getting the drinks and snacks out of the machines was taking so long that the attendant came over and opened the front of both machines so that we could reach in and take what we wanted. It was a sight to see Mr. Jones, Jack, Mike, and Bruce walking out with their arms full of bags of popcorn, Cracker Jacks, M&Ms and cheese crackers. We walked back across the street to the tire dealer, sat down on the grass or front steps and started eating.

A short while later, our bus returned. We reloaded and hit the road. While we had been waiting, Rosanne Miller (Mr. Jones' assistant) had located a Trailways charter bus in Harrisburg, Pennsylvania that would take us home. Adam agreed to make the 4-hour drive to get us there. I think they had even convinced him to take us all the way to Louisville if we had been unable to make other arrangements. At least we had a way home.

Midway through the journey, we had to leave the expressway to get gas. We were somewhere in rural Pennsylvania when we pulled up to the gas station. They did not have any diesel fuel. We drove to another station, which also did not have diesel fuel. The attendants there thought a station about five miles down the road would have some. We headed off down the little two-lane road enjoying the countryside and hoping to make it to the station. We had traveled only a couple of miles when we spotted a station that had a sign that proclaimed "We have diesel." It was a welcome sight.

Everyone got out to stretch their legs while Adam was refueling. Gene Shields proved that he can do windows by finding the squeegee and going to work on our bug-splattered windshield. Spirits had lifted considerably and we took a group picture before reboarding for the remainder of our journey.

At 9 P.M. we finally pulled into the Trailways bus facility in Harrisburg. Along the way, we had missed a couple of turns and had taken a circuitous route around the emergency room drop-off circle and parking garage of a local hospital. The bus facility looked deserted. There were very few lights on. We pulled up and waited. Someone noticed a cloud of exhaust coming from a bus at the rear of the lot. In a moment it had pulled up alongside the garage. We got out and began transferring our luggage.

While most of us stood near the rear of the Crystal Tours bus, Adam was surrounded by Mr. Jones, Mike, Jack, Jacque Sokolov, Bruce, Ken and Tom. We watched as they were negotiating the price of the trip—repeatedly reaching into their pockets to see if they could cover the cost. Adam was very considerate and did not take advantage of the situation. They finally settled on a very fair price of $150 per person, which came to a total of about $3,500. Dr. Sokolov was the only one with a decent amount of cash and paid for the largest part of the tab. Mr. Jones wrote Adam a check for a very nice tip. We said our good-byes and Adam headed back toward New York City.

The Trailways bus was like a luxury liner compared to our little Crystal Tours bus. Everyone had a large reclining seat to themselves and an empty one next to them where they could stretch out and relax comfortably. Our driver pulled out of the facility at 9:30 P.M. and began looking for a place to eat. Unfortunately, all of the eating establishments that we passed in Harrisburg closed at 9 P.M., even the fast-food places. We got back on the expressway and headed west.

After about an hour, we reached the end of the expressway. A short three-mile trip would get us to the Pennsylvania Turnpike, which would take us to Ohio. It was here that we found a restaurant that was still open called Eat 'N Park. We had a wonderful dinner. The service was excellent. The food was served quickly. And we enjoyed the first really relaxing moment of the day. As we left, the restaurant staff gave us a big bag of cookies to snack on as we traveled through the night.

We reboarded the bus, settled into our seats and began nodding off to sleep. Some remained awake and carried on quiet conversations. Some could be seen sitting quietly, lost in their thoughts, as they stared out the windows into the night. We took a rest stop near the Ohio state line in the middle of the night, and stopped at a McDonald's in northern Kentucky for breakfast.

Mike purchased the remaining copies of the USA Today newspapers that were stacked on the counter. As we ate, we passed around the various sections of the paper and read about the events that continued to unfold in New York. The photos were enough to break your heart, especially the ones of those who chose to leap from the World Trade Center before it collapsed. I just wanted to fold up the newspaper, give it to someone else and walk back to the bus. Reminders were not needed. The images would not be easily forgotten, no matter how hard you tried.

The remainder of the trip passed very quickly. It seemed that in no time we were pulling up to the HAC facility in Louisville. It was 9 A.M. It had been a very trying 24 hours and we were thankful to be home. Everyone left the bus and collected what remained of their luggage. The departures were swift and without any fanfare. Transportation arrangements to get home were made, good-byes and thank-yous were said and in only moments, everyone had scattered. Everyone was looking forward to a hot shower and a few moments of quiet solitude.

I walked into the Humana building just before noon and found that quite a few of the group had already returned. We would all spend the next few days repeating our stories. It seemed that everyone wanted to hear about our experience and express their gratitude that we had returned safely. Some wanted to talk to someone who had actually been there in an effort to understand what had happened. The concern for our welfare was most heart-warming.

I keep telling people that I am grateful to have missed the immediate danger area by scant minutes and that I am glad to be back home. But it is not always the truth. There are many moments when I would rather be back in New York, digging through the rubble to help recover those who unfortunately did not get out before the collapse. I know that there will be many that will never be accounted for. I know that there are many that have lost loved ones and will never get past their grief. Most will eventually return to a somewhat normal life, if it can be called that. But many more will bear emotional and physical scars for the rest of their lives. It is only our love, compassion, and emotional support that will sustain them.

Today, as every other day, life goes on. It is up to us, individually and collectively, to make it a better life for all so that this kind of tragic event will never happen again. If possible, to remove the reasons that would cause anyone to ever consider such a tragic course of action. Only then will we feel truly safe again.

View of the smoke, near the New York Stock Exchange, after the second plane crashed.

SEPTEMBER 11 MEMORY

Denise Damron

The image that continues to replay itself over and over in my mind is the view outside the back of the van as we left our hotel at the World Trade Financial Center and turned the corner off of West Street at about 8:40 A.M. on September 11. An explosive blast ripped the top off of the World Trade Center, sending large pieces of what looked like white confetti twisting in the wind, slowly spiraling down between the tall buildings. As we moved further down the street and around the corner, the tower came into view again, flaming debris and glittery glass plummeting down faster now.

My first thought was that a bomb had gone off. Then the sound of sirens filled the air as emergency vehicles began to make their way through the crowded streets. I see it all now as a movie in my head, except that instead of watching the movie, I am in the frame and the events are all very real.

As we arrived at the Digital Sandbox and got out of the van, people walking down the street seemed unaware of the explosion. But soon after we arrived, I physically felt a tremor followed by a loud boom. More pieces of flaming debris immediately began floating through the air, along with a sooty, sandy grit that showered down like snow. Looking down the street towards the World Trade Center, the smoke and debris blasted toward us like water bursting from a dam. I turned to see people running away from the blast, covered in the grime.

We were watching TV in the lobby of the Digital Sandbox when I learned that a plane had hit the north tower of the World Trade Center. I thought it was a tragic mistake. How could a plane hit the building? When we heard that a second plane had hit the south tower, a feeling of dread and disbelief overtook me—I realized that this couldn't possibly be a mistake. Frantically, I tried over and over again to call my family on my cell phone, but the calls would not go through.

I think we were all immobilized in the lobby, glued to the television, until Diane Davis and I decided to go up to the fourth floor. This is where our product launch was to have been held that morning at 10 A.M. There obviously would not be an event now. As more of our group made their way to the fourth floor, our first thought was to contact our families to let them know we were all OK. Miraculously, phone lines appeared, thanks to the management staff at the Digital Sandbox.

I finally got through to my family, assured them that we were OK, and told them I'd call back later when we knew what we were going to do. The more I watched the CNN broadcast on television, the more horror I felt for the people in the buildings. When the south tower collapsed, I felt a deep involuntary sob well up from my chest. I don't recall at that time feeling any fear for myself or for our group. My only thoughts were for the people in the buildings and fear that our entire group was not yet accounted for, worried that they might possibly be in or near the fallen buildings.

As our team gathered around the television, we heard the news broadcaster say that a third plane had hit the Pentagon. Then, in what seemed like mere seconds, we heard that a fourth plane had crashed outside of Pittsburgh. Shortly thereafter, it was announced that the north tower had collapsed into a heap of rubble. I think we were all stunned and bewildered—was this the beginning of World War III? Who was attacking us and why?

Shortly after the buildings collapsed, I looked out the window of a nearby office and saw nothing but thick black smoke pressing against the glass. When I walked into the empty hall by the elevators, I smelled a smoky, gritty substance and felt that I was breathing in soot. My eyes began to burn and my breathing became labored. It was at this moment when I first began to feel fear. For a fleeting second, I thought that we may be trapped, suffocating in this building.

Looking out the window in one of the meeting rooms, I could see blue sky beyond the top of our building. The smoke seemed to be rising from the sidewalk and making its way up. Even now I can't forget the image down on the street below—the sidewalks, the street, cars, building signs, and people covered in a thin layer of sandy-colored dust.

I know I made several more calls to my family to reassure them that we were OK. Most of the time, I don't recall feeling in any real danger. I always felt that we would leave the building when the smoke cleared and make our way out of the area to Midtown. However, I distinctly remember not being able to watch the television monitor that was broadcasting live the chaos that surrounded us. Again, the horror of the people who were in the towers overtook me and my eyes would become watery with tears.

At one point, sitting on the window sill in the meeting room I looked down on the deserted street and saw what looked like a homeless woman shuffling along the sidewalk smoking a cigarette amidst all the swirling soot. I remember feeling incredulous that she could possibly be inhaling a cigarette while obviously breathing in grit from the exploded buildings.

From the view out the window, the streets were empty except for a few police officers wearing masks and helmets walking through the intersection on the corner. The scene didn't seem real. And it certainly didn't feel like we were literally in the midst of all of it.

Fear began to grip me again when I heard that the police were asking people in our building and surrounding buildings to leave the area immediately because of the possibility of gas leaks. The most surreal moment for me came when we began ripping up tablecloths to use to cover our faces as protection from the smoke. Until that time, I felt that we were safe and insolated in our own little building and I resisted within myself about having to leave.

Our group quickly mobilized, gathered all our belongings—laptop bags, suitcases, briefcases, whatever we could carry—and descended to the building lobby where a guard directed us out the back door to a side street. I remember stopping to put on my sunglasses because my contact lenses began to feel gritty. Diane and I were at the back of our group as we made our way through the silent, empty streets. I felt that I had witnessed this scene before—perhaps in a film—or had read it in a book: "The refugees trudged onward, carrying all their belongings, fleeing the war-torn village . . . " There was no sound, no wind, only sirens in the distance.

After walking for maybe 30 minutes through the sandy streets, we came to a cordoned off intersection, blocked by police barricades. Suddenly, the sun was shining, cars were honking horns, people were scurrying about their business as if they had no awareness of the horror that hovered only blocks away.

The rest of the story of how we made our way out of New York and back to Louisville 20 hours later has been recounted numerous times. Driving out of the city, the image out the back of the bus was of a cloud of black, billowy smoke. The city suddenly seemed so small and fragile.

It is only after returning home to "normalcy" that I have realized what was truly unfolding around us as we were cocooned in the Digital Sandbox during the morning hours of September 11. I think not only of the tragedy of the people who died in New York that day, but of myself and our group and how blessed we were to have made it through. I've felt a great amount of pride in how we rallied together and, with great determination and stamina, made it home to our families and friends.

There is a certain bond that developed among our group. I can only imagine it must be like the bond that is forged among soldiers in war who witness unspeakable atrocities yet somehow make it through on sheer conviction and will. While I know that most of us did not actually see the area around the buildings and the rescue efforts that went on, I believe we were all affected in a profound way.

I feel a certain amount of isolation from family and friends when it comes to the events of September 11. I can't begin to describe to them what it was like and how it felt—and still feels. About how tears come unbidden at every memory, every news report, every thought of those who lost their lives. I can't listen to people in the grocery store talk about the incident without wanting to scream, "You have no idea what it was like." I can't bear to watch video footage or see newspaper photos of the buildings without seeing fiery debris floating to the ground. I can't look at these images without putting myself on the street when the first plane struck and remembering the feelings of helplessness and horror. Only in talking to those who were there can I take comfort in knowing that others are feeling the same sense of separation.

I recently developed a roll of film that was in my camera—film that I had intended to use to take photographs of our grand event in New York City. I had forgotten that on the morning of September 11, at about 8 A.M., I looked out my 33rd floor hotel room overlooking Ellis Island and snapped two pictures. The day was sunny and clear and full of the promise of our exciting new venture. How the world has changed since the moment I snapped those pictures.

THIS CHANGES EVERYTHING

Diane Davis

Tech analysts from Towers Perrin, American Express, Renaissance Interactive, and ADP were scheduled to "get a front row view of the future" as the cover of the CD-ROM invitation promised. Inside the invitation a card read, "Change happens. September 11, 2001." Humana Inc. had plans to make an exciting announcement about a new online health insurance product called Emphesys on Tuesday, September 11, in Lower Manhattan. All the big executive and media dogs from Oracle, The Wall Street Journal, Reuters, Cisco and other companies had made plans to witness this revolution— something the consumers, doctors and employers craved—health insurance without all the hassles.

New York was selected early in the plans because it made good business sense to announce something revolutionary on Wall Street. Fortune 200 health insurance company, Humana Inc., developed an intelligent online health insurance product that promised to change everything. And there is no doubt that in a new dawn, it will. To win in the game of high-tech Internet functionality, you have to be the first to announce your product to the right people, at the right time, at the right place. September 11 in Lower Manhattan was carefully selected with this goal in mind and all the cards were falling into place.

I was asked to assist in the production and planning of the New York product launch. We had completed a successful kickoff meeting in Memphis, Tenn., for enthusiastic insurance brokers on August 22. So, there was no reason to expect failure in New York.

With success a cinch, I grew anxious for the trip while packing, despite tears and a plea from my 13-year-old daughter Lauren not to go to New York "just because." But I was excited to be part of the project. It had all the makings of something huge for Humana. Excitement overshadowed the telepathic behavior my daughter displayed. Perhaps as a distraction, I asked Lauren and her twin sister Caitlin to find something to attach to my corporate black computer bag, making it easily distinguishable from the rest. They proudly selected a brilliant yellow plastic plucked chicken key chain, complete with red beak and comb. It lacked corporate decorum, but my kids selected it, therefore it would remain.

Brief morning clouds had burned off and September 10 was shaping up to be a beautiful, bright day in Lower Manhattan, without an ounce of nasty eastern humidity. After a 9 A.M. conference call with the others in Louisville, Denise Damron and I ventured toward the Digital

Sandbox, taking a sightseeing detour through Wall Street. We made a couple of wrong turns, but were able to see an exhibit outside the New York Stock Exchange. There were shiny new Lincoln Blackwood cars and a hospitality tent. Denise told me that the NYSE allows the companies sponsoring the bell start for the day's trading to have a display. I brought my personal camera and the company's digital camera and took photographs of the Lincoln exhibit.

Set-up at 55 Broad Street took forever. It was well after noon by the time we left for lunch. Dick Brown suggested a quaint café he had seen down the street called Vine. As we walked to lunch, it felt good to be outside in the sunshine with the New York people. We passed a building with a street sign advertising a play called "The Last Castle." The graphics were intriguing and caught my eye. The sign featured an eerie image of a tall medieval building with smoke billowing out from behind it. An upside down American flag was also proudly displayed.

After lunch, we headed back to the Digital Sandbox. The afternoon went quickly and before we knew it, we were preparing for Tuesday's launch at a 5:30 P.M. rehearsal. Things went well. Particularly memorable was the emotional closing statement of our president Mike McCallister: "From this day forward, nothing remains the same. This changes everything."

Time was money, and our senior-most leaders had exclusive dinner engagements that evening at the top of the World Trade Center in the Windows on the World restaurant. Their guests were health policy leaders, large group employers and technology presidents. Rumor had it that everything went well. They enjoyed themselves so much that they closed down the bar. Of course none of us could have imagined then that this would be the last dinner served at Windows on the World.

Those of us not dining on top of the world were tired, hungry and glad we weren't taking part in the dinner festivities. Leaving the rehearsal Monday evening at around 7:30 P.M., we were surprised to step outside into a heavy downpour. Some of us cursed the weather and wondered how it might affect our carefully laid plans. (During our journey out of New York the following day, my mind kept going back to this wet evening. I believe this sudden downpour was a burst of tears from heaven and an expression of the horror soon to follow.)

Early Tuesday morning on September 11, I pulled back the curtains of my hotel room in hopes that the dreary rain clouds had passed. They had, and another Kodak moment was upon me.

Nervous energy had me running through the day's details in my mind. I visualized success for us on Broad Street. I shrugged off the ridiculous thought that something bad would happen to distract the media attention we deserved. I never fathomed that someone else might be visualizing their own success much more strongly than I.

By 7 A.M., our senior leaders had left the Marriott World Trade Center to be driven to several pre-event media interviews, each falling into place like over-ripe apples in early fall. Our president appeared on a Bloomberg interview at the American Stock Exchange that ended at 8:45 A.M.

The rest of us were scheduled to meet in the lobby of the Marriott Financial Center at 8:30 A.M. for van transportation to the Digital Sandbox three blocks away. The vans were running late and pulled up at 8:40 A.M. Our backs were to the World Trade Center as we headed away from the hotel. While waiting to turn, we heard a loud noise that sounded like an explosion. We looked to pedestrians for signs of concern, but people on the streets didn't seem bothered by the bang. So we shrugged it off as common occurrence, a typical New York sound. It wasn't until the van started to turn that Ken Fasola caught sight of a yellow ball of fire protruding from a tall building. He screamed and pointed upward. We barely caught a glimpse of the horror before tall buildings blocked our view. Reams of white paper were shooting out of the fiery hole in the building and hanging motionless in the air. As the driver moved ahead, he glanced toward the cause of our hysteria and shouted into his radio, "It's the World Trade Center! There's been an explosion!"

I thought by now that passers-by would have noticed us in the van pointing upward with wide eyes. But they didn't. I grabbed my camera and captured the scene on film. Sirens screamed past us as my cell phone rang. It was Mary Sellers calling to say we were cancelling the media interviews and we were to meet at the Digital Sandbox.

At this point, we were only a half a block away from our destination, but slowed by emergency vehicles blaring around us. I took another photograph of the burning building and ticker tape-like projectiles floating in slow motion. (When this photograph was developed the next day, I learned I had captured a flying object banking in a circle near the flaming tower.) People on the streets didn't seem to know what was happening.

Just before we got out of the van at the Digital Sandbox, I called our president's assistant, Janice Seaman, and told her that she may hear about an explosion in New York on the news. I wanted her to know all of us were accounted for. I also called Christine Van Ormer, our marketing department assistant, and told her that there had been an explosion at the World Trade Center. I wanted her to spread the word that we were all OK and would gather at our original meeting place.

As I entered the Digital Sandbox with luggage in tow, I scanned the small crowd gathered in the lobby in hopes of finding others from Humana. People were staring with wide eyes and open mouths at the large television screen capturing the unfolding events. Word quickly spread that a hijacked plane had hit the north World Trade Center tower. My first emotion was sadness at the loss of the many innocent people on board the plane and in the tower. As I turned to see what was happening outside, another boom sounded. People in the lobby screamed. A second hijacked plane had just hit the World Trade Center. My body shook fiercely as I backed myself against a wall for support. Several people began weeping openly.

As people cried at the TV footage of the second plane careening into the north tower, I went outside to be with two coworkers. Frightening words were being tossed around like a salad. "Terrorist attacks." "Transportation closed." "Thousands of lives."

My camera finger, albeit shaky, was itchy to capture more images and I needed a distraction. The smoke was outrageously white and billowy thick. Although I wanted to, I opted not to photograph the fear in the faces of people who were gathered on the sidewalk staring toward the smoke of the burning towers. Instead, I pointed the camera upward and captured smoke coming from behind the tall buildings. In the frame, the American flag waved proudly in the forefront. People began moving quickly down the middle of the street. Many people glanced toward the sky behind them as they walked rapidly ahead.

Most cell phones, especially those relying on Sprint, weren't working. But my Powertel phone was operable. I called my husband Ron to tell him I was close to the towers, but would be all right. He didn't seem to understand the peril I was in, so I decided not to make matters worse by describing the scene. He called other spouses to notify them that their loved ones were accounted for. He later admitted that he had no idea how close I was to the Trade Center at the time.

Within minutes of the second crash, people had become more frantic. Several began running. A man shouted to a guy next to him, "Let's get the hell out of here." As I watched them run away, someone grabbed me by the arm and pulled me inside the building. I wished I had noticed who had pulled me from the sidewalk so I could thank them. Immediately thereafter, burning debris landed in the place where I was standing.

Inside the lobby of the Digital Sandbox, a large crowd had their eyes fixed on the television. Since I didn't immediately spot people from our group, I took the elevator to the fourth floor where our presentation was supposed to occur. I found a handful of our team members gathered in a meeting room just as another thundering sound sent shivers down my spine. The lights in the building blinked. Building security personnel requested that everyone move immediately to the basement. By now, word had spread that the first tower collapsed and the second was in danger of doing the same. This was the first time I felt my life was in peril. Together with our president and chief innovation officer, we made the decision to obey the voice and proceed down the stairwell to the basement. Weighed down by the luggage and laptop I refused to separate from, I pulled off my heeled dress shoes.

In the basement, I felt imprisoned. It was too quiet and there were few Humana people with us. My mind panicked. I suddenly realized that I had not asked anyone to call my children at school to let them know I was okay. At that moment, I would have given anything to hold and kiss them. I made a promise to God that if He let me live, I would go back to church faithfully, rebellious children and all. It wasn't long before Mike suggested we go back and get the food and water on the fourth floor. We all jumped at the chance to leave the basement and left behind our beloved luggage.

When we reached the fourth floor, we piled water and orange juice bottles onto tablecloths that we could carry over our shoulders. Within moments, a large contingent of our colleagues appeared. Together, we decided to stay put on the fourth floor, because some of the phone lines actually worked.

Sam Garas had set up his laptop and had been able to connect his modem. He let me use his e-mail to send a message to my kids. Off the top of my head, I could only recall the e-mail address of a business partner who knew I was in New York. I asked Sally Matteson to call my children's school with word that I was all right. I quickly sent another cryptic message to my mother to deliver word of my safety in case family members called.

In the meantime, our group had managed to stake out a private room. There was a television and some working phone lines, though most were in constant use by others. Our food and drinks were placed in a room nearby to share with the other 75 or so people who were stranded with us on the fourth floor. The room had windows, which allowed us to see what was happening in the deserted, dismal streets.

Not long after we had secured our position, it dawned on me that I had left my belongings in the basement. I decided to run back to the basement to retrieve my bags. As I ran down the stairwell, another loud rumbling jolted the building and the lights blinked again. I was pretty sure the sound had come from the collapse of the second tower and I prayed it was not falling on top of us. For a second, more intense time, I felt my life was about to end. This feeling grew when a security guard opened the door to the first floor, sending clouds of smoky brown debris into the stairwell. The guard shuffled two, maybe three, dazed people covered in gray dust into the stairwell. I continued down the stairs through the clouds staving my panic. Once in the basement, I saw heaps of corporate-black suitcases piled on top of one another. My eyes glanced toward the area where I had left my bags. It wasn't hard to spot the bright yellow chicken hanging off my computer bag. I smiled through teary eyes thinking of my children. I grabbed my bags and hoisted myself up the stairs one final time. The air near the first floor smelled like burning metal combined with another scent I could not describe. I had to cough as I ran up the stairs.

Back on the fourth floor, I glanced toward the windows that appeared to be covered by dark brown drapery. Looking closer, I noticed it was not drapery but turbulent clouds of debris that instantly darkened the room. I watched TV footage as people struggled for air. Footage of the damage done at the Pentagon was gut-wrenching and the stink of pulverized concrete hung near the elevator doors. At different times, I was asked if I was all right. Apparently my face was bright red and I was hyperventilating. I forced myself to sit down and drink water using the hand that was shaking the least. I watched the people who were talking on the working phones and willed them to get off. When someone finally hung up, I scrambled quickly to call my husband. I felt a need to say I loved him and was not sure when, or if, I was coming home. He said he was optimistic knowing our group had vowed to stick together. I doubt he understood that I was trying to tell him goodbye forever.

When it was apparent we would be in the building for a while, I decided to change into my University of Oregon T-shirt, jeans and tennis shoes. If we had to flee the building, I would be able to move quickly.

The staff at Digital Sandbox was fantastic. They made sure we could hear the news unfold and replenished our beverages often. They also announced that two doctors were stationed in the basement if anyone needed assistance. After a while, my heart rate returned to normal. Even my cell phone began working. I contacted my mom who was talking to my brother on the other line. Both were worried about my safety. I assured them we had been through the worst and planned to leave the city soon. It was a good thing I called her after I had calmed down, because she isn't easily fooled.

A Humana employee in Louisville called my cell phone, crying with worry about our safety. She wanted assurance that we were all right and begged to do something for us from Louisville. Though I was confident that a fellow employee had cancelled plans to join us in New York, I asked her to confirm his whereabouts and call me back immediately with an update. She called back and said I had nothing to worry about. He never left for New York. I thanked her and told her she was a tremendous help and comfort.

The leaders in our group were trying to locate transportation out of what was quickly emerging as a death zone. The area where we were sheltered had been barricaded from access and was at the edge of what the media termed "Ground Zero." All modes of transportation in and out of the city had been halted. Airports were closed and the buses and subways weren't running. They grounded all of our company's corporate jets at the airport for an undisclosed period of time. Ferries were only taking the injured to New Jersey hospitals. We tried to locate rental vehicles available anywhere close to New York. I called my dad, to hear his voice and to get my Uncle Albert's phone number in New Jersey. Uncle Al said he would roust up cousins and uncles with cars and meet us wherever we landed in New Jersey. I passed this information along to others to throw into the rescue pot of ideas. Even though we did not end up using the "Italian Brigade" escape plan, I felt comforted by Uncle Al's willingness to do whatever it took to rescue my Humana family and me.

Efforts to find transportation out of Lower Manhattan did not look good. Our chairman Mr. Jones offered his New York apartment as a second base camp once we got out of Lower Manhattan.

Our group began to grow. With those of us from Humana were advertising agency vendors and guests who were in New York for our event. These included people from the Northlich Agency in Cincinnati and Hill-Holliday in Boston; Phil Johnston from Renaissance; Steve Lieber, CEO of HIMSS; and Larry Atkins from Washington, D.C. Some made plans to find their way out of the city on their own. Others opted to stay with us.

It was close to 2 P.M. when word spread that a possible gas leak created a threat of fire to the building. We had to hustle, whether we were ready or not. It didn't take long for our group to huddle in a corner like a mob of frightened meerkats awaiting direction. The plan was to head toward the Hudson until we thought of something better. I saw Anthony Choate cutting a strip of tablecloth to use as a makeshift face cover. This cloth cutting process appeared arduous and he did not have enough cloth for everyone. I pulled down a sheet of black drape from our display, and began cutting strips quickly with scissors borrowed from the Digital Sandbox. While grabbing the scissors from the assistant, I remember telling her to "bill us" for the damaged linens. I asked Eileen Hutchison to douse each cloth with water because it seemed like the right thing to do.

Once everyone was outfitted with a breathing cloth, we moved quickly and silently downstairs to the first floor. The giant screen television in the lobby that once projected unbelievable news of terror was stone cold silent. The clean, clear glass wall that once opened up into a bright street filled with fast-paced human activity was covered with a brown curtain of crud and dust. We quickly took roll call, assigned ourselves a "buddy" and were reminded of our vow to stay together. The security guard escorted us to the back door where he bade us good luck. The door opened onto a New York street covered in inches of concrete dust and who knows what else.

Although I have never been a refugee, I now know what it must feel like. Everything looked gray, except for the brilliant red, white and blue colors of the American flags that hung weeping over the streets. It was bittersweet to leave the shelter of the Digital Sandbox, but I knew that my allegiance to my newfound family was stronger than any desire to stay at 55 Broad Street. I would probably have followed them to the edge of the world if they had asked.

I trailed behind the cluster because I felt the need to take photographs of our escape. The streets were practically void of people. What few cars remained on the streets were covered in soot and parked. A New York Police Department van had all of its windows blown out. Every once in a while, a couple would walk hurriedly past our group without saying a word. Several of us in our group had black carry-on luggage with wheels. The view from behind the group was surreal: a pack of people walking with their heads bent forward, with knotted fabric strips hanging down the backs of their heads like Lop rabbit ears. Little puffs of gray soot shot up from the wheels of each piece of luggage. I pulled out the digital camera to capture the moment. In my haste to keep up, I mistakenly placed the camera on the wrong setting and missed capturing an image on film that only our group will forever remember. And it was not until then that I noticed the camera had been set on the wrong date mode the entire trip.

Those who had assumed the lead in our group finally revealed a plan. We would walk several city blocks toward the East River. Hopefully by that time, we would hear from an assistant that a bus had been secured for our return to Louisville. If necessary, we could have a slumber party at Mr. Jones' New York apartment until another plan jelled. In the meantime, we had to circle around the perimeter of Ground Zero before reaching the bay.

As we approached the site of monumental devastation, there was silence. Everyone was quiet as if out of respect for those who had lost his or her lives. Images flooded by. A woman's stylish black shoe lying on its side in the middle of the street. One single men's shoe. A piece of a man's yellow tie. It was the piece just below the knot and above the bottom. Both ends were shredded, not cut. Business papers were strewn everywhere and covered in gray soot.

As we cleared the area, everything went from monochrome to Technicolor. The air was sunny and clear. There was far less soot in the streets. More people populated the sidewalks, but they weren't talking much. Most amazing to me was the extraordinarily loud chirping of the birds. They were either very happy, or very angry. Regardless, their sounds were a pleasant distraction from the hell we had just left behind. One I shall never forget.

Somewhere near Oliver and Madison Streets, by the grace of God, we happened upon a Crystal Tours bus. The engine hood was up and the driver was leaning against his vehicle. Bruce approached Adam, the driver, and said "we'll make it worth your while" to get us out of the area. After a brief discussion, Adam agreed and we loaded suitcases into the back. I found it necessary to take another photo of the smoke just before we loaded ourselves onto the bus.

Somehow the bus fit our entire group of 30, with room for a couple more. Mr. Jones befriended an elderly lady on the street who looked upset and offered her a seat. It turned out she was a 1948 graduate of the University of Louisville. Small world.

It was a quiet ride through the busy streets of Chinatown as we headed toward Times Square and out of the city. My friends laughed at something above my head—the chicken key chain on my luggage was swaying happily to the beat of escape. We dropped off a couple of our associates who had relatives nearby and our special U of L alumni guest. During our bus tour, I saw two men walking down a crowded sidewalk wearing Israeli flags across their shoulders. A news photographer followed closely behind taking photographs of their proud march.

Somewhere between 20th and 87th Avenues, a cell phone brought good news. A Trailways bus had been found and was being held for us in Harrisburg, Pennsylvania! Adam willingly offered to drive us there. The drive toward the George Washington Bridge—the only bridge left open to traffic leaving New York—was painfully slow. We saw many, many police cars and ambulances screaming toward Manhattan. As we slowly moved across the bridge, I was overcome with a sense of relief. I tried calling my husband to give him my whereabouts, but they had evacuated the Federal building where he worked. I left a message on our home machine and looked forward to calling my children after school.

We made our way into New Jersey and past the airport. Somewhere near Milburn, we heard the pop of a flat tire. For some reason, this was comical to me and didn't seem to phase anyone else either. Adam commandeered the injured bus across several lanes of NJ Expressway traffic to the tune of angry car horns and near collisions. Some in our group felt as though THIS was the closest they came to death.

Ironically, our chief information officer knew Milburn, New Jersey quite well. He gave Adam directions to a tire store from the freeway off ramp. We stopped to stretch our legs, search for food and find restrooms. It was beautiful in Milburn, but there was no food to be had. Mr. Jones walked across the street from the tire store to a miniature golf course. He bought out all the snack foods and sodas in the vending machine. I'll admit those were the best peanut M&Ms I had ever, ever tasted.

Anxious to get to Harrisburg, we piled back on the bus and headed for the expressway. Adam noticed the gas gauge was leaning toward empty. He asked our CIO if he knew where to find a diesel station. Sure enough, we found one and quickly gassed up the chariot. There was just enough time for Ken Fasola to take a group photo.

Back on the expressway, Adam asked if we wanted to watch the news. Nobody wanted to, so he put on a video. The movie that played was the stupidest I had ever seen. We were glued to it and whooped and hollered at the ridiculous humor. I was sitting next to Dick Brown. We kept looking at each other wondering what was so funny. It felt good.

After several hours, the sun looked as though it was going to allow September 11 to finally end. The landscape in Pennsylvania was so peaceful. We were all quiet.

We arrived at the Trailways station in Harrisburg sometime around 10 P.M. It was time to pay Adam for the chariot ride out of hell. If I had a million dollars, I would have given it to him. Mr. Jones and the others huddled together like they were playing football.

Adam left with a grin on his face while we loaded up the spacious bus for an all night ride home.

Because we were famished, the driver took us to the Appalachian Microbrewery. Just our luck, they had stopped serving food. We bought up the beer in the cooler to stave off our hunger. That was the best pale ale I had ever tasted! Further down the street we found an "Eat 'N Park" restaurant (similar to a Denny's). We took over several booths in the restaurant and ate contentedly. The waitress asked where we had come from, and we explained. When it was time to leave, she gave us a bag full of cookies with frosting smiles.

Back on the bus, we were anxious to hit the road home. We would be driving straight through the night and expected to get into Louisville at 9 A.M. Heidi Margulis had bought vodka in New York, and she divvied it up in cups with ice from the restaurant. Dr. Jack Lord distributed Tylenol PM to anyone in need. Everyone needed at least one of the two concoctions, and most opted for the Tylenol with vodka chaser in hopes of a complete slumber. Not many on the bus actually slept. After about an hour on the road, I got on my knees and peered over my seat at the people behind me. When my eyes adjusted, their bright smiles told me I wasn't the only one who could not sleep.

It was almost 7 A.M. when we arrived in Florence, Kentucky and saw the golden arches of McDonald's restaurant beckoning us like a lighthouse on choppy waters. The cashier let us in. Mike slapped money on the counter and said, "Feed 'em." We ordered, then read the morning papers that Mike had bought. It was ominously quiet as we read in horror about what had happened in New York. Had we really been there? Half the group read each word intently. The other half, myself included, began to read, but had to stop. My eyes watered and I couldn't read another sentence or look at another photo. I folded up the paper, and tried to hide my tears as I ate breakfast. Hopefully the leaders didn't spot my weakness. When I saw a few trying to hide their grief behind opened newspapers, I knew they weren't all reading the paper either. These people were just like me after all.

The senior-most people gathered in the front seats to lead us into the home stretch. Some clapped and others quietly cried when they saw the Louisville exit sign two hours later. The bus took us to the airport where most of us had left our cars. When the bus doors opened, everyone scrambled quickly to their cars with very little to say. Mr. Jones kindly thanked us individually for our help. Other than that, nobody had anything else to say to each other. We were family now, and that changes everything.

Everyone, including the bus driver, had left the area except me. Ron was supposed to pick me up, but he got lost finding the air corporate building. Thank God, because it gave me a chance to enjoy the sunshine, cry a little, and listen to the birds chirp again. They didn't sound angry to me.

Diane Davis

Broad Street after the collapse of the first tower and seconds before the sky became totally black. Despite its appearance, the photograph is in color and properly focused.

ALMOST NEW YORK

Judi Farmer

It's Sunday, September 9th and I am unpacking suitcases from my just-completed vacation, washing clothes and trying to pack for New York and Memphis. It's going to be a busy week starting tomorrow and I won't be back home until Thursday, so I am trying to pack efficiently. I call Marcia and find out that many of the Humana folks are flying up to New York today and the rest are going on the corporate jets tomorrow. I will be going to New York on a commercial carrier by myself. I decide to go into the office on Monday morning to catch up on the mountain of emails that must be waiting and fly in the afternoon.

My flight on Monday leaves Louisville on US Air around 11:30 A.M. and goes through Washington. I am in Washington and am concerned because weather is moving in to the East Coast. Sitting in the shuttle to New York, we are lined up and ready to take off when the pilot comes on and says that we are delayed due to storms in New York. Over the next four hours our plane taxis back and forth at least three times between a resting place and the runway. It's now 6 P.M. and the pilot says that the flight is cancelled altogether and taxis back to the gate. Every hourly shuttle to New York has gone through the same routine and the airport is pandemonium. We are told that we are on our own—so many people rush to try to get to Amtrak and others try fruitlessly to get hotel rooms. I decide to go back to Louisville tonight—it just isn't in the cards for me to get to New York.

I call Marcia to tell her my plans and to see if there are enough people to man the kiosks in New York. My plan is to meet everyone in Memphis. When I find out that Dave George cannot attend because he broke his foot and Bob Wittenmyer was stuck in North Carolina, I feel I must get to New York the next morning. After booking my flight back to Louisville, I call the travel agency to book an early morning flight to New York. I tell the agent that I need to get there early in the morning and she says, "You're in luck." There is an early morning direct flight from Louisville at 6:45 A.M. It's perfect, so I book the flight, then fly back to Louisville.

I awake to my alarm clock at 5 A.M. on Tuesday, September 11th. I'm tired, but I know that I have to get to New York. So I cut it a little close getting to the airport, but I still have 15 minutes to spare. When I get to the US Air desk, the agent tells me that the flight is leaving—RIGHT NOW! I protested, "But it is supposed to leave at 6:45, can you get me on it?" He looks me up in the computer and says, much to my surprise, "You are not even booked on this flight, you are booked to go to Washington Reagan at 6:45 A.M.!" I find out that I do not even have a ticket to New York at all. While I am busy cursing under my breath at the travel agent that messed up the night before, I have to purchase a new ticket so I can get to New York. Now with a connection in Washington, I won't even land in New York until 10 A.M. Since the kiosks are not supposed to be manned until around 11, I decide to try it. I have to run to the very last gate (of course!) to catch my flight to Reagan.

I manage to call Marcia Jaggers from the runway in Louisville before departing to Washington to tell her what has happened. "I'm coming one way or another Marcia, I may miss the entire thing, but I'm coming to New York and I'll see you there." "Maybe you'll see me," she says (rather prophetically). "No, I'll see you today," I affirmed. I am determined to get to New York. I ask where the Digital Sandbox is located and she says, "It's near the World Trade Center."

We take off and the purr of the engines quickly coaxes me to sleep. I am jolted awake by the announcement that we are landing at Reagan. I look at my watch and it's 8:15 A.M. So far so good. The weather is perfect and it's still quite early, so flights should not be delayed. I get into the terminal and board the next flight to La Guardia, scheduled to depart Washington at 9 A.M. I'm sitting in my seat thinking, "Okay, this is going well. I'll make it to the Digital Sandbox in time, I know I will." We taxi out to the runway and the pilot comes on and says that we are sixth in line for take off.

A few minutes pass and the pilot comes on again. "Folks, there is a problem in the New York sky, and we will be delayed. We won't know anything for about two hours, so we are going to taxi to a resting spot and you will be able to use your cell phones." Talk about déjà vu! I couldn't believe I was hearing about a delay once again. So I turn on my cell phone to call Marcia, and it immediately starts ringing. It's Brandon, my 23 year old son . . . "Mom!" he cried, "Did you hear the news? A plane hit the World Trade Center in New York! Isn't that where you are going this morning?" I reply "We are going to be somewhere near there. Oh my God, I hope everyone from Humana is okay. Let me get off and call Marcia."

As soon as I hang up, there is a voicemail for me from Marcia, "Judi, apparently a plane has hit the World Trade Center and it's on fire. I don't know what is happening yet, so call me when you get this message." I try to call Marcia, but her cell phone is busy. My phone rings again, "Mom, a second plane has hit the other tower of the World Trade Center!" I couldn't believe my ears. Again I try frantically to reach Marcia with no luck. I try Sam Garas, but his cell is busy too. I'm looking up other phone numbers when the pilot comes on: "Folks, the airway over New York is closed, we are cancelling this flight today." We taxi back to the terminal and I deplane and get in line to get a ticket back to Louisville. I finally get up to the desk and begin to book my flight home when an airport representative comes around and says very calmly, "We are evacuating the airport. Please take your things and move to the nearest exit."

There was no panic and no real sense of urgency, but I decide to comply. As I am walking out I look over my right shoulder and see thick black smoke rising over the hill. "What is it?" we ask each other, but no one seems to know. Everyone is sort of dazed. We walk past a bar with television sets and people are watching the news from New York. I am outside milling around near the building with everyone else when an FAA representative comes out and calmly states, "A plane has hit the Pentagon. Please move back from this building until we can determine that it is safe to go back inside."

We all slowly move back toward the parking lot. I try my cell phone again—no luck. The circuits are jammed. They move us back into the parking lot. Some of the flight attendants from United are crying. I keep trying my cell phone over and over. Finally, my phone rings. Again it's Brandon, "Mom, one of the Trade Center buildings collapsed." I am in shock and I'm really worried about everyone from Humana. Did they get out okay? Just how close are they? I try to call work over and over to see if Jenifer Burke has heard anything. Finally I reach her and she tells me that they are all safe. Thank God, I thought to myself.

Over the next hour or so, the FAA representative periodically moves us away from the terminal, up and down large grassy hills and toward the George Washington Expressway that separates the airport from Crystal City, Virginia. The air is laden with black smoke, but we can breathe and see where we're walking.

I have started talking with a couple of women. One, Pat, is a convention manager from the Seattle, Washington Visitors Bureau. Elizabeth is a lobbyist for the American College of Physicians and the Society of Internal Medicine. We obviously can speak the same language and immediately hit it off. Elizabeth lives in Washington, but they are evacuating and she is not allowed to try to cross the city to get home. So the three of us decide to look out for each other. We chat and try to reach our families by phone, but the cell lines are jammed. Some people around us are crying and some are looking dazed. One woman with an FBI hat is acting a little strange—she is alternately trying to tell everyone what to do and crying.

The FAA rep comes over again and tells us we have to cross the highway, which is bumper to bumper with traffic fleeing south. We start to cross and get to the median where there is a concrete embankment about four feet tall running the length of the highway, followed by two metal guardrails and another concrete embankment. By this time I have changed into flat shoes from my suitcase, but I am wearing a long straight skirt and dragging my bag behind. I am eyeing the obstacle course in front of me, unsure of how to negotiate it when a kindly person appears from nowhere and lends a hand. I have been clutching my cell phone the entire time trying desperately to get a line, so I stick it in my pocket, hoist my skirt and clumsily flail myself over the median, only to be faced with the frantic traffic fleeing the city. My guardian takes my hand and helps me run across the highway where I meet back up with Pat and Elizabeth. Unsure of where to go, we move under some trees. It seems the safest place to be.

Most people are remaining calm and the traffic, while heavy, appears orderly. Someone starts to beep his horn when the rather unstable lady with the FBI hat starts to yell, "Hey buddy, lay off the g . . . d . . . horn!" The guy in a red sporty type car stops right in the middle of the highway, gets out and starts yelling at the FBI-hatted lady, who is yelling back. It's a startling sight. Finally a policeman and a pilot emerge from the throng of people and settle them down. The horn blower gets in his car, shoots an obscene gesture and leaves.

Before we can really react, an FAA rep appears with a bullhorn and shouts, "There is a hijacked plane making its way back to Washington. It's about ten minutes out and the US is going to try to shoot it out of the sky. You are not safe here, you have to leave right now!" Elizabeth, Pat and I look at each other and try to assess our options. Fear is finally setting in. We obviously can't go back to the airport and we are backed up against Crystal City, a concentration of skyscrapers built of concrete and glass. Going there doesn't seem like such a good idea. We begin to walk down the highway. I decide to try to reach my family again, only to discover that my cell phone is gone from my pocket, most likely lost in the median. I feel like a refugee after a war, aimlessly ambling away from somewhere but toward nowhere, dragging my belongings behind me.

A flight attendant says "Follow me, I know how to get to Crystal City from here." The three of us looked at each other. We are all thirsty, tired and in need of a restroom at this point, and even with reservations about Crystal City, we decide to follow.

Around 11:30 A.M. we come to a Marriott hotel in Crystal City. The lobby is teeming with other airport refugees sitting around watching events unfold on televisions. The bellman allows me to call my husband and tell him I am okay. Ivan tells me that my son has called my brother who lives in Baltimore, and asked him to come get me. However, the major highways in Baltimore and Washington are all closed. I try to get a room at the hotel, but they can't tell me anything until 6 P.M. So we sit and watch, and sporadically try to contact loved ones.

By 5 P.M., Elizabeth reaches her daughter who says that parts of the Metro (the Washington subway) are open again. Pat has a friend who lives in Virginia and she decides to take the subway south, while Elizabeth graciously offers me respite at her home in Northwest Washington. We take the Metro to within a few miles of her home. However, the Israeli embassy is right near her house, so we walk a great distance around the embassy to get to her home. It feels like it's uphill the whole way and I vow to start an exercise program once I get home.

I finally reach my brother and tell him that I am in Northwest Washington, a place that is much easier to reach from Baltimore. "Please come get me." He agrees and sets out for Elizabeth's house. Later in the afternoon a friend of Elizabeth's comes over. She works at the Capitol and tells us her story of being evacuated. She says that the secret service grabbed some of the senators and took them to the basement, but many fled the building alongside other workers. We all were transfixed on television for several hours.

My brother, Ken, shows up around 8 P.M. Many roads have reopened and the cell lines are freeing up. I decide to try to reach the Humana folks on Ken's cell phone. Marcia's phone must be turned off so I try Sam. He answers. We are both on cell phones and the lines are not clear. "Where are you, Sam?" Tears are filling my eyes. I know he's safe, but he's the first person in the Humana party I am able to reach. Sam tells me he's at his sister's apartment in New York and the Humana folks were able to flag a bus to get out of town. I am trying to tell him about Washington, but the line is breaking up and I lose the connection. The floodgates open—I guess the emotion of the day finally got to me.

After I reach Ken's house in Baltimore, I call Ivan and Brandon and tell them I want to come home right away. We make arrangements for my brother to drive me part of the way, to Clarksburg, West Virginia, and they will meet us there and drive me home. On Wednesday morning (it seems like a lifetime has passed), Ken and I head out for Clarksburg. We plan to meet at a Hardees restaurant. We drive for several hours, then pull in to the restaurant and go inside. Within five minutes, Brandon and Ivan pull up. Again my tears begin to flow.

On Thursday, I call Marcia because I feel a strong need to see her. On the way I purchase a new cell phone, which seems like a necessity to me now. Marcia opens her door and we hug through the tears. We talk for a couple of hours and I know I feel better after seeing her.

A few days have passed and I am coming in the door on Saturday when the phone rings. It's Brandon. "Mom, you won't believe this. I just got a call from a man from upstate New York— he found your cell phone!" He apparently went through my address book on the phone and finally found a number that had an area code attached to it and called. I took his number and called him back to thank him for going to so much trouble to find me. He told me that he hooked up with a man from Virginia who took him to his house when the Metro opened, then drove him home, all the way up to Elmira, New York the next day and would not accept a cent in return. He felt he needed to do something as well. I received my cell phone in yesterday's mail. If these acts of kindness spread, perhaps there is a reason or a silver lining to this national tragedy after all.

The events of September 11, 2001 have left lasting impressions with individuals from around the globe. Our proximity to the tragic events in New York and the experience we shared over those next twenty four hours have left me with several lasting images. Let me share three I replay frequently in my mind's eye.

The view of a rain-soaked New York City seen through a lightning-filled sky from the top of the World Trade Center as Mike McCallister, Jack Lord and I prepared to greet our guests for dinner. Twelve hours later that building was gone.

Looking up at the World Trade Center towers just three blocks east as Eileen Hutchison commented on what a beautiful day it was and seeing the first explosion from the other side of the impact, not yet knowing it was caused by a commercial aircraft crashing into the building. As the sky filled with paper which began landing around us, some still burning, we had no idea what was about to unfold.

As the building we were in began to shake from the impact of the first World Trade Center tower collapsing, day turned to night and the air inside smelled of smoke and pulverized cement. Those few minutes, when rumors of additional explosions circulated throughout the building, appeared the most stressful for our group.

Looking at the enormity of the loss so many individuals experienced, our trip home now seems more like an inconvenience than an escape from harm's way. Yet, an "experience" it was. The unselfishness and cooperation shown by the entire Humana team in New York was an inspiration as are the company's actions in support of those in need since our return.

God Bless America and all those who have lost fathers, mothers, family and friends. Our thoughts and prayers remain with them.

Photo: Diane Davis

A view of Broad Street from the fourth floor as riot police secure the streets after the collapse of the towers.

AUTUMN IN NEW YORK, SEPTEMBER 2001

Sam Garas

There is nothing better than autumn in New York. Although it was technically not fall yet, the weather was gorgeous and the sky that we could see through New York's skyscrapers was a cloudless blue. On the last day of my combined business and pleasure trip, I was lamenting the fact that I would be leaving New York. I hoped that my trip could be extended for a few more days. You should always be careful what you ask for.

We started Emphesys, Humana's new digital health plan, almost two years ago. I joined in May of 2000 with the great hope of using technology to revolutionize the health care industry. Revolutionize may be an overstatement for health insurance, but this was Humana, one of the best companies to work for in Louisville, and I was given a chance to develop something new from scratch that nobody had done before.

I started getting involved in the New York event shortly after our successful Memphis broker rollout in August. I was really looking forward to going to New York. I traveled to the city many times, mostly to visit my sister who went to school at Columbia and was now working as an attorney in Midtown Manhattan. The event was on a Tuesday and we needed to set up on Monday. That gave me the opportunity to spend the weekend in New York visiting my sister and becoming a New Yorker, at least temporarily, once again.

Sunday night saw me heading for the Marriott Financial Center Hotel in downtown Manhattan. I arrived at the hotel and went right to my room and ordered room service. I was exhausted from the long weekend and wanted to get some rest. I knew the next two days would be hectic, I just didn't know how much.

Monday morning was again a beautiful day. The hotel was only a few blocks from 55 Broad Street, the site of the Emphesys presentation, so I decided to walk. The walk went right down Wall Street and the streets were filled with people all trying to get to their office for another week of capitalism in action. I was in awe of the sights and sounds as I walked fast so I would blend in just like any other New Yorker. A few minutes later I found our presentation building and I went to the fourth floor. I was the first to arrive. Others arrived shortly afterward and we starting setting up the hall for the presentation we knew would be exciting.

The setup went smoothly and we waited for all the senior executives to arrive for a dry run. They all arrived on time and went through the presentation several times. The presentation turned out much better than I could have imagined. The production company we hired really went all out and this was truly something different from just a new health insurance product rollout.

After finishing the practice sessions, we were all hungry. Many senior executives went to the restaurant at the top of the World Trade Center. I gathered another group and we got a couple of cabs and headed for the China Grill in Midtown Manhattan. My sister recommended the China Grill and we met her there. We all had a great dinner and did not feel guilty about the size of the bill, which will forever remain confidential.

After dinner at the China Grill, several of my colleagues mentioned that they had never been to New York before. We took the opportunity to walk off dinner by going to Times Square and again getting the full New York experience. We enhanced the experience by taking the subway back to our hotel. The subway took us to the World Trade Center where we walked back to the Financial Center hotel a couple of blocks away.

Tuesday morning arrived and revealed another glorious day. I met several co-workers for breakfast in the hotel restaurant. I also waited for a few people from Workscape, a vendor we used to help develop the Emphesys Web site. I convinced a group of people to check their bags and walk to 55 Broad Street. Having done the walk the day before, I knew how great of a walk it was. The weather also made it an easy decision to walk. We checked our bags in the lobby and headed out.

Once we arrived at the presentation site, we went to the room and made sure everything was still working OK. Everything was fine and we anxiously waited for our invited guests to start arriving. Someone quickly ran into the presentation room and shouted, "We have a problem, a plane just hit the World Trade Center!" We thought he was crazy. How can a plane hit the World Trade Center, the tallest buildings in New York, on such a beautiful day?

We quickly went to one of the computers that were hooked to the Internet. We went to cnn.com and sure enough, there was a picture of one of the World Trade Center buildings on fire. I gathered a few people and went outside to see what was going on. We got to the sidewalk and saw smoke just rising out of the World Trade Center. We knew then that our presentation was over. We knew that people would start evacuating the area and that it would be impossible to go forward with our event. We were disappointed, but at least we were OK and felt safe where we were. After trying to make several calls on my cell phone, I heard an explosion followed by people screaming and running down the sidewalk. Paper started falling on us and we felt like we were in the middle of a ticker-tape parade. That paper quickly turned into bits of steel and I quickly went inside the building I came out of.

At first I thought the explosion was from the building that was on fire. I soon found out that another plane hit the second World Trade Center building. I realized this was no accident and knew that this was deliberate. I didn't panic and everyone from Humana stayed calm as we watched the events unfolding on television. We were lucky enough to have power in the building and we were well informed on what was going on. We all felt safe and we accounted for everyone in our group.

As the hours unfolded, the situation was getting worse and worse. The Trade Center buildings eventually collapsed and a sea of soot and darkness covered our building. We stayed calm, but I was starting to question the wisdom of staying where we were. It became a moot point because we had to stay put until the dust cleared from the towers' collapse.

As we waited at 55 Broad Street, I was able to get in touch with my wife, mom, and sister. I had invited my sister to join us at the Emphesys presentation. Luckily, she was running late, as usual, and she heard about the planes hitting the towers before she got on a subway to downtown. She was safe in her apartment.

The phone lines were almost impossible to use during the tragedy, but I got in touch with my wife a few hours after the first plane hit. She was obviously relieved to hear from me, but I made the mistake of telling her that "I'm covered in soot!" I meant to say that the building we were in was covered in soot, but that we were fine inside the building. She started to break down as she realized how close we really were to all that was going on. I calmed her down and reassured her that everything was going to be all right and that our group was getting ready to make it out of the area.

As we headed out of the building, the dirty snow of soot covered the streets and presented a surreal scene. We kept walking past blown out cars, broken glass, and emergency vehicles heading toward the collapsed towers. We finally made it out of the area and our group was able to find a tour bus guide willing to use his bus to take us back to Louisville.

I got off the bus around Times Square and started walking towards my sister's apartment on the Upper East Side. The bus continued on and eventually made it back to Louisville with everyone safe. I was stuck in New York for a couple of days before finally taking a limo to Philadelphia, renting a car, and driving back to Louisville.

It's hard to explain all the emotions you go through after a tragedy like New York. All the experts will tell you what you should be feeling, but you cannot really know unless you experienced it. I think most of us that made it out safely keep asking ourselves why we made it and so many thousands of others did not. We could have been the ones sitting in the hotel having breakfast, getting off the subway, eating at a restaurant, or just walking down the street when the tragedy took place and not have made it out alive.

We of course did make it out alive and have to be forever grateful for that. Our continued purpose may be taking care of our family and raising our children, or it could be a greater cause that we now have a chance to fulfill. Whatever it is, we will all be looking for that light that leads in a direction to complete a mission given to us by safely walking out of New York.

*B*ruce Goodman, CIO at $10 billion health care company *Humana Inc., is a witness to history.*

Goodman was part of a group of senior executives from Humana, including CEO Michael McCallister, and vendors Oracle Corp. and Electronic Data Systems Corp., who had flown to New York Monday to talk about a new Internet project. The group was to meet Tuesday morning at the Digital Sandbox, a high-tech presentation facility near the World Trade Center. There was no meeting. Instead, Goodman and his colleagues were incredulous witnesses to the terrorist attack on the Manhattan landmark, choking on dust clouds and seeing scenes of horror that are only now beginning to sink in. Goodman is unhurt and back home in Louisville, Ky. He shared his story with Kim Nash of Computerworld.

Q: Tell me about what you went through. You were in New York to do a presentation.
A: We might have been the last people to eat at Windows on the World. The night before, we were there. About 30 of us in a private room on the 107th floor of the north tower.

Some people were staying in that Marriott hotel that was just at the base of the World Trade Center towers. Fortunately, they were over at the meeting at the Digital Sandbox when it all hit. They lost their luggage. That was the only thing they lost.

One person from Oracle wound up getting blinded by the collapse, by a dust cloud. He was helped out of harm's way by some New Yorkers who took him in and helped him get to an ophthalmologist later on.

There were also some EDS people with us, including one who just became head of [EDS's] health care vertical unit. He was a doctor. He set up a first-aid station in the basement of 55 Broad Street.

Q: Where were you when the attack started?
A: Some of us were out walking on the street trying to get a bagel that morning. It's funny, we made a choice when we got to the World Trade Center not to go into the little shops there. Had we done that, we would have been in there when the first plane hit. But we had turned right and gone into another store.

I didn't hear the first plane. We were on the street when the second plane hit. It was really eerie. You saw enormous clouds of smoke and all this paper settling down, some of it still burning [when it got to] the sidewalk. You could sense that paper was part of people's lives and part of civilization. And it was all going up in smoke. It's hard to comprehend. People were just standing with their hands over their mouths, eyes wide open. It was total shock. We can't believe this was happening. We can't believe this is happening so close to us.

Q: What happened then?
A: We retrieved some luggage from the cars we had nearby. We were seeing emergency vehicles going in and knowing an hour later they were trapped under rubble and weren't coming out.

The [Digital Sandbox] building we were in, it became a shelter for people. We had ordered food and drinks for the meeting; it was in there already. It was very, very difficult breathing [through] the dust from the first [tower] collapse. I don't know if you've ever seen a building during a controlled implosion, but there's this enormous cloud of dust that envelops the whole site and rolls out like a wave. That cloud of dust completely engulfed everything in a 10-block radius. When you looked out of windows and doors, it was as black as night. It looked like someone painted the windows with black paint.

You see Hollywood disaster movies where there is panic and people run. Here, people were moving fast. They had fear in their faces but were under control. They weren't panicking and screaming. If someone fell down, someone else picked them up. The banding together was just incredible.

We set up a TV to watch what was going on. All these people were on the street, and we were taking them in, and they were taking advantage of the food and water and coffee and first aid. We saw the buildings come down on CNN, and we felt the ground shake in person. The smoke alarms went off, and the lights dimmed. You were watching it on TV and feeling it, right there, so close.

Q: You're safely back in Louisville now. How did you get out?
A: We were there through 2 P.M., after both towers had collapsed and the third building was threatening to. I never feared for my own life, perhaps naively so. Though if the fumes got too thick in our building, we could have suffocated. But it all didn't seem that real to me.

Our cell phones were out, but we had landlines. I have a son in New Jersey who was trying to arrange for rental cars, but I couldn't call him directly. I had to call through Louisville, and they called him and he called back, like a relay. Our corporate headquarters was working on our contingency plans, too. We were pretty much in constant communication. Our CEO was getting messages back to headquarters and telling our people not to worry and to go home if they felt upset. Being active like that really let us focus on the practical side of things and not let our emotions get in our way. But when we got home, I felt terrible—the horror of what we'd seen.

At 2 P.M., we had ripped up tablecloths to put over our mouths. This was all very surreal. The impact doesn't get to you until it's over. Anyway, we had all of our wheelie luggage, and we took attendance on the ground floor and established a buddy system. Each person was responsible for two other people. We just vowed we were going to stick together and walk out of there and stay together and solve this as a group. We really bonded.

We went out a back door of the building to the street. Have you seen those science-fiction movies about the day after a nuclear holocaust? It was downtown Manhattan and everything was coated with at least half an inch of pan-gray dust. There was no traffic. There were 26 of us, marching orderly in the middle of the street. We were going east, so we could make a wide circle around the World Trade Center, then head north. There was no one else out.

The dust, as we're walking along, is getting kicked up just by our walking. Everything is a monotone color. It's so surreal in terms of what we're doing. We're moving along and trying not to kick up too much dust.

There was a police car on the sidewalk with its windshield totally smashed in. In the distance, we see an emergency vehicle coming toward us, lights blinking. It goes by us and raises a huge cloud of dust.

Then it's as if you changed the channel on a TV. The scene changes. It goes from monochrome to color. There are thousands of people on the street, emergency vehicles, a light-blue sky, which you couldn't see before. You can't believe you just walked away from this ground-zero scene.

Q: Where were you walking to?
A: We knew people who knew people who had apartments, and we were going to try to stay over or hook up to some rental cars farther out of the city. Then we came across a tour bus parked with the hood up and the radiator steaming. We talked to the driver and found out that he wasn't out of commission. So we said, "Are you willing to take us somewhere? We will pay." He was willing. We were lucky. We had 26 people, and he had 30 seats. We piled in. I was

talking to him, and he was willing—not initially, but eventually—to drive us back to Louisville, if necessary.

[On the way,] we met a woman who was a social worker and had just seen [a client] and asked us for a lift. She was in her 60s.

At the same time, we had people in Louisville working on potential bus connections. They managed to secure a charter for us in Harrisburg, Pa. This fellow drove us all the way to Harrisburg. We got a flat tire in New Jersey.

From the time we left ground zero at 2:00, it was 19 hours until we were back in Louisville, 700 miles away.

Q: What was going through your mind during all of this?
A: None of us panicked, though when we finally got home, people let their emotions out. The horror. You walked and saw all this debris. We saw a men's tie neatly shredded into four pieces, lying in the street. All these papers just scattered. It was an incredible message about the threat to our civilization. A mindless, maniacal act.

Q: How do you feel now?
A: Relieved and angry. Angry. Frustrated. And hoping that our government is going to see this for the serious long-term threat it is and take appropriate action. Given what this portends in terms of future significant events, we have to wipe out terrorism. We are going to have to give up some of our civil liberties for the mutual protection of everyone. I'm willing to spend a little more time [in security checks] at airports if I'll be safer.

I'm thinking about the complacency and arrogance we have as a country. Hopefully, this is enough of a wake-up call so no one else has to suffer like they have [at the attack sites].

Q: Will you undergo crisis counseling?
A: No, I'll watch myself. I have a hard time watching TV. The things you see—how touching and how horrible. I don't think I have any lasting effects, other than I won't get those images out of my head. You see such a contrast between the horror people can do and the wonderful good you feel for fellow human beings in trouble. The contrast is the most incredible thing.

(Reprinted by permission from *Computerworld* magazine.)

Police van on Pearl Street in the financial district, its front window smashed by falling debris.

DEAR
FRIENDS
AND FAMILY

Marcia Jaggers

This has certainly been a week to remember as we mourn the loss of lives and share grief as a nation. But I wanted to share my story of hope and good news amidst all this chaos.

I think I've been in NYC twice within the past twenty years, and Tuesday, September 11 was one of those dates. I was about three blocks from the WTC when the first tower was struck. One of about 30 associates from my company, I was in NYC with a team to demonstrate our new digital health plan—I've participated in its development over the past 19 months. On Monday night, half of our group stayed at the Marriott, about a half block from the WTC (including myself), the other half at the WTC Marriott. Several others held business dinners atop the trade center restaurant the night before. On Tuesday morning, we left the hotels by van about 8:30 and were on Battery Street when the first plane hit the north tower. The fire and smoke were immediate; fortunately, we were not outside for the unfolding of the remaining tragic events during the next five hours.

Within minutes, our group gathered indoors at the Digital Sandbox, on Broad Street, about five blocks from the towers, where we had expected to host the meeting for an audience of about 100. This is probably one of the most wired locations in NYC—we had kiosks with e-mail access, ready outbound availability of phone lines, and large-screen televisions with CNN reporting. The building retained its electricity/air conditioning and we had the comforts of a full food spread because we had set up for a large gathering. My luggage was with me throughout (several had checked theirs at the hotel) and I had even packed spare casual clothes at the last minute (including some flats!) before leaving home.

We could *hear* the sounds as the buildings came down, *smell* the smoke (even inside the building), and through the windows *see* the smoke and ash covering streets and cars. The outside air was thick. We were able to stay in the building until about 2 P.M., when police began encouraging people to move north. We tore up the tablecloths to serve as nose/mouth breathing filters and headed out into the streets rolling our luggage. Stepping into the streets felt like a nightmare, as we could literally *taste* the ash in the air. There was debris everywhere, including papers on the ground—many with project plans and timelines. Smoke billowed over the entire city. Our plan as we left the building was to walk about five miles to an apartment of one of our associates' daughters—but God provided a different plan. We walked about a mile and found a driver outside his empty tour bus, with seating capacity for exactly 30 (the size of our group). He agreed to drive us out of the city. With only one bridge open, it seemed like it took over two hours just to get out of the city. Once outside the city, the tour bus was taxed to its weight and speed capacity—we blew a tire, but suffered only a temporary delay while it was repaired. This tour bus driver took us all the way to Harrisburg, Pa., where we were able to get a charter bus to bring us into Louisville. We arrived home safely about 19 hours after leaving the building in NYC. It was about 9 A.M. on Wednesday morning.

Amidst all this turmoil, it's wonderful to know that God is still in control. I'm not sure why I was there on this date, but I know that the experience has given me a renewed appreciation for guardian angels and it will change my perspective on priorities for a lifetime.

—Marcia

NEW YORK CITY — SEPTEMBER 11, 2001

David A. Jones

Several people have suggested that I record the events of September 11 in New York, as I saw and participated in them. So, even though you have already heard my story, I'm writing it for possible future reference.

Betty (Mrs. Jones) and I returned from Ireland on Sunday afternoon, September 9. Monday the 10th was a routine day, with a little jet lag, and an afternoon decision by me to fly to New York City early the next morning in order to attend the national announcement of our new digital health plan, called Emphesys.

It was scheduled for 10 A.M. on the fourth floor of the New York Information Technology Center, 55 Broad Street, in a special venue called the "Digital Sandbox," a fully wired environment. Invited were financial analysts from technology and health insurance sectors, health and technology news media, and Humana director Mike Gellert, who works on 42nd Street in New York.

I left Louisville at 0600 on 733-M, arriving at LaGuardia at 0730 and at 55 Broad Street at 0830. Being a bit early, I bought a cup of coffee in the Starbucks shop on the ground floor of 55 Broad Street and was drinking it when the first plane hit the North Tower at around 0840.

We all heard what sounded like a huge explosion. I looked up and saw people running south on Broad Street, away from the World Trade Center (WTC), which was three or four blocks away.

Shortly thereafter, I spotted our president and chief executive officer, Mike McCallister, and his team approaching 55 Broad Street from the north. They had left the American Stock Exchange, where Mike had given a Bloomberg TV interview, just before the first plane hit, and were showered by debris as they walked very near the WTC en route to 55 Broad.

Some of the presenting group, which included vendors like EDS as well as Humana employees, had stayed the night before in the Millennium Hotel, a part of the WTC. Mike and his team had also hosted three dinners that night at Windows on the World, atop the WTC.

I then joined them and shortly thereafter we entered the Technology Center, where a huge TV screen, perhaps 20' x 30', was obtaining real-time feeds from a news helicopter which showed the second plane as it approached and hit the South Tower. At that point we all knew that something real and terrible and tragic was unfolding.

We joined our colleagues in the Digital Sandbox on the fourth floor of 55 Broad and began trying to call loved ones to say we were okay. We also sought to find hotel rooms as it became clear that all area airports would close. Cell phones didn't work for awhile because of the intense traffic but landlines did work, and we made our calls, but had no success at all in obtaining hotel rooms.

I told Mike, Jacque Sokolov and Jack Lord about our apartment at 69th and Madison, and that we could put up the entire 23-person team there for awhile, until the situation clarified.

There was some concern that other planes might hit our area, but that dissipated as time went on. Then the South Tower collapsed, and a huge ball of black smoke, dust and gunk filled the streets in the area, causing real concern about the air supply and possible smoke inhalation. I was prepared to suggest that we make a run eastward to the East River if air quality in our building deteriorated. Luckily, the air handling system worked well, although some smoke did come up around the elevator shafts.

We learned later that Mike Gellert came up out of the subway just as the South Tower collapsed, and was enveloped by that terrible cloud of smoke and dust. He reported that he tried unsuccessfully to outrun it, then ducked first into a Starbucks, then into a building where he found refuge in a third floor laundry where he stayed until the smoke cleared enough to allow him to walk Uptown to his 42nd Street office.

Before long, the North Tower collapsed and we had a repeat of the enormous smoke/dust cloud, which kept us pinned down.

At around 1:30 P.M., I suggested that a few of us go down and check the streets, especially the air quality. Jacque and Jack joined me and we found a policeman and asked if we could try to walk north. He said yes, but that we would first need to walk a couple of blocks east, to stay well clear of the WTC area, which was a scene of total horror and where hundreds of rescue workers had been trapped as the two towers collapsed.

We returned to the fourth floor and asked everyone to prepare for the walk north. We had in the meantime heard through my secretaries, Rosanne Miller and Debbie Alexander, that one of our pilots, Paul Urbahns, was at his daughter's apartment on East 25th Street and could accommodate six people. So, my plan was to drop six people, those least able to walk a long way, at the 25th Street apartment, then continue with the rest to my 69th Street apartment, hoping at the same time that we might find some public transportation operating as we got farther north. The subways were definitely closed and we were pretty sure that public transport was unavailable.

Before starting our walk, we initiated a "buddy" system, three people to each group, charged with assuring the presence and safety of their buddies. My "buddies" were Bruce Goodman and Jacque.

Several of our colleagues found tablecloths and cut them up for use as masks. They were really helpful, as passing emergency vehicles stirred up the dense dust that filled the streets. Bruce, our chief information officer and former worker on Wall Street, guided us with remarkable skill, and we soon emerged from the danger zone into beautiful weather but a chaotic scene of dazed, unbelieving people moving northward.

After walking only 25 minutes, we came upon a 28-seat tour bus, parked empty on the street, with the driver working under the raised hood. I asked him if he could drive us north to 69th Street with a drop off on 25th Street. He hesitated, saying that there were police roadblocks. I told him we'd handle those and that we could and would make it well worth his time to take us. So he said yes and the 31 members of our party, 24 from Humana and seven vendors, piled in, with luggage and with one other passenger.

She was an older woman also walking north, from a social work meeting where she had been trapped, as had we. It turned out that she was a 1948 graduate of the University of Louisville Kent School of Social Work. I'm sorry that I don't know her name.

Once aboard, Mike and Bruce began to broaden the driver's charter, asking whether he could take us all the way to Louisville. When he found out how far it was he declined, but faced with the superb negotiating skills of our team, and the promise that we'd "make it worth his while," he agreed to take us as far as Philadelphia, where we thought we could charter a bus for the remainder of the trip.

Rosanne and Debbie in Louisville were working on the bus charter. Bruce was working the phones, Mike led the negotiations and I sat beside the driver and showed him where to drop various passengers as we made our way slowly north.

As we crossed the George Washington Bridge at 4 P.M., there were 24 of us left, 22 Hummers, one vendor, Steve Lieber, from Chicago and an invited guest from Washington, Larry Atkins (who left us in Harrisburg). A few minutes later, a rear tire blew out, but there were dual rear tires, so we made it to the next interchange in Union, New Jersey. Bruce had lived in New Jersey, so he directed our driver to a tire shop, which didn't have our size, then to another one which did. Steve Moya stayed with the bus to protect valuable luggage, and the rest of us descended on a convenient golf driving range, which offered toilets, water, soft drinks and nibbles, since no one had eaten since breakfast. With a new tire and diesel fuel found by our New Jersey hero, Bruce, we set out for Pennsylvania. No buses were available in Philadelphia, but Rosanne and Debbie had arranged a Capital Trailways charter in Harrisburg and that's where we headed.

At this point I want to mention the teamwork and solidarity that prevailed from the first indication of danger to our arrival in Louisville. Each individual acted with strength, grace and dignity, even though many had significant personal concerns. Several of the young women had children in school and difficult child care arrangements to achieve. Diane Davis had a digital camera, and cheerfully documented our activities. If memory served, I would try to name all the many acts of resourcefulness and kindness performed by our team, but I would surely omit some so won't try. I do want to record the fact that our hosts at the Digital Sandbox were remarkable in their sensitivity and capability in providing space, phones, water, information and encouragement.

At 9 P.M., right on schedule, we rolled into the lovely, riverside city of Harrisburg, which had been suggested by the two Pennsylvanians among us, Ken Fasola and Luisa Charbonneau, as a place where we might charter a bus, after our efforts to find one in Philadelphia failed.

With Ken's help, we quickly found the Capital Trailways bus depot and a larger, more comfortable bus waiting to bring us to Louisville. As people stretched and luggage was loaded, Mike asked our New York driver, a cheerful and helpful Hispanic fellow named Adam, what he thought would be a fair price for the trip from Lower Manhattan to Harrisburg. He was in a perfect position to take advantage of us but did not do so, suggesting an extremely reasonable price of $150 for each passenger. His attitude echoed that of everyone with whom we connected on that tragic day. He was helpful, he was kind, he was capable and he did not try to take advantage of our plight.

Even so, we had to come up with $3,500 cash, so we all opened our wallets and purses and chipped in. We learned that Humana executives seem to rely on their credit cards, as most of the wallets were pretty thin. However, our esteemed consultant, friend and highly experienced world traveler, Jacque, had a handful of large bills. We soon relieved him of them, and I'm going to recommend that we repay him, if he can present a valid receipt! Having contributed my ready cash, I wrote Adam a personal check for $1,000, as a gift honoring his selfless act of friendship.

Our Capital Trailways driver found a nice place to eat, called Eat 'N Park, similar to a Big Boy, at around 10 P.M., and we all ate well, with lots of milkshakes and double burgers, our first real meal since breakfast. At 11 P.M. we boarded our comfortable bus, with two seats for each of us, and settled down for a good night's sleep. That was sort of guaranteed by our thoughtful and well-prepared physician, Dr. Jack Lord, who offered everyone except yours truly (who was already asleep) a Tylenol PM and a taste of an unnamed liquid relaxant. I can't speak for the others, but I slept soundly until a pit stop near Columbus, Ohio, then slept again until being awakened in the parking lot of a McDonald's in Covington, Kentucky, where we ate a fast but delicious breakfast. Reboarding, we arrived at HAC, where most of our cars were located, at 9 A.M.

While we were all heavyhearted and filled with sorrow for innocent victims, we maintained our composure and sense of humor and my colleagues were all wonderful traveling companions.

Those Humana associates present throughout the saga were: Dick Brown, Luisa Charbonneau, Anthony Choate, Denise Damron, Diane Davis, Ken Fasola, Bruce Goodman, Eileen Hutchison, Marcia Jaggers, David Jones, Marsden Kucera, Brian LeClaire, Jack Lord, Heidi Margulis, Mike McCallister, Steve Moya, Tom Noland, Mary Sellers, Gene Shields, Fred Smart, Jacque Sokolov and Bob Wittenmyer. Beth Bierbower walked with us and rode the bus as far as 42nd Street. Sam Garas left the bus near Times Square. Steve Lieber, CEO of vendor HIMSS, was with us all the way to Louisville.

People leaving Lower Manhattan after the air began to clear.

SEPTEMBER 11, 2001

Marsden Kucera

How exciting! How grand! The time had finally come
Emphesys was real and the world was going to know
We were all in New York—I was so excited I was numb
We celebrated from the top of the world with the city below

The morning was clear and we were ready to go
With enough extra time to grab a bagel or a treat
So walking we went following Bruce the pro
To the deli, not the tower, because of my sore feet

The next thing we knew the unbelievable occurred
A plane hit the tower and showered debris
We saw the destruction but couldn't believe what we heard
Another plane hit, we were under attack—that couldn't be

I'll never forget the faces of shock and disbelief
The overwhelming feeling of complete disarray
The devastating loss brought on a great sense of grief
But my thoughts went to my family who were too far away

As I stood on the street talking to my husband John
I heard a loud explosion and screams of shock
There was another attack the terrorists weren't done
Then came a tidal wave of dust rushing around the block

I ran for my life, truly thinking my end could be here
I reached the door of the Sandbox and made it inside
Just as we were plunged into a world of darkness and fear
Then discovered the cause and could not imagine the number
    who died

As my senses returned I realized our predicament
Survival instincts kicked in and emotions were sedated
I saw all the people that shared my confinement
And was thankful for each one as we waited

Our thirst for knowledge was so strong
We sat and watched the news unfold
But no matter the explanation—it was still so wrong
There was no comprehending the story being told

With leaders committed to doing something—to act
We left our building with trepidation and scarves around our neck
We encountered a world that caused my heart to contract
Walking through a nuclear fallout was how we started our trek

Then I encountered the things that hit me so hard
The personal belongings of people who were at work just like me
The realization of the lives that were forever marred
And the family celebrations that would never be

I couldn't wait to see my children and have them caressed
But I needed to cry first and finally let out the grief
And I realized I was not only lucky but truly blessed
With family and friends and a new-found belief

God gave me an opportunity thousands didn't get
To make a difference with my life and be the best I can be
I'll never forget that day and feel an incredible debt
To those who sacrificed to remind us what it means to be free

I will remember September 11, 2001, as the day I was . . .

Stunned that such a heinous act was conceived of, nonetheless committed.

Saddened that so many people lost their lives and loved ones.

Faced, no matter how briefly, for the first time in my life with my own mortality.

Witness to the truest meaning of teamwork.

Comforted by those around me.

Concerned about those not with me.

Changed forever.

Lucky.

THANK YOU!
BRIAN LECLAIRE

Dust and smoke continue to fill the air at 2:15 p.m. near Ground Zero.

THERE
IS NO
CONTROL

Jonathan Lord, M.D.

For months a team of excited and dedicated people worked to build a "first": an all-digital healthplan, the first leg in our efforts to transform health benefits in America. Part of the team's charge was to develop a launch strategy that would be both national and local in scope, that would reach the media and key stakeholders and that would provide a template to "re-launch" and invigorate the new Humana. Team members along with leadership went to Memphis in August to meet with brokers in the market and to test the message. We learned a lot there; the need for clear graphics, integrated message, scripting and driving a message of change. From late August through September 10, there was a daily "war room" around preparation for launch week . . . everything from details around logistics, to media lists, to development of scripts to new graphics and video testimonials. That team did a truly splendid job in an amazingly short time. By the time we got to New York on September 10, we had a really great production that was set to "revolutionize" the world. We had rehearsed several times in Washington and in Louisville . . . a team arrived in New York on September 9 to make sure that everything worked . . . and we drilled and re-drilled the presentations in dress rehearsals at the Digital Sandbox on the evening of the 10th. I remember feeling that we had really done it . . . a first-rate presentation that would transform the world, and in the words of the song "New York, New York" . . . if we could make it there, we could make it anywhere. In retrospect there were some real ironies to the presentation. We opened with a scene of the power of people exemplified through taking down the Berlin Wall. Throughout the presentation we made reference to revolutions . . . how revolutions are driven by people . . . and how our premise for change was built around the notion of giving information to people to allow them to direct their care and destiny. Our script ended with a line of "I promise you . . . today will be a day that you will never forget."

Energized from the rehearsal, we went to dinner at the World Trade Center in two beautiful private rooms. Our guests ranged from leadership from our business partners, to national health care leaders to local leaders influential in healthcare policy. I remember the dinner vividly, since I had selected the menus . . . evaluating each dish against the options I chose from. It was a good night. On the way back to my hotel, I spoke to my friend and partner Alice, recounting the day and sharing the excitement about our launch on September 11.

Tuesday morning . . . and early up . . . and a wake up call from Alice at six wishing me well for the day. Words of encouragement and praise for what we were about to do. The first team of folks, Mike McCallister, Bruce Goodman, Tom Noland and I left the hotel at seven to go to the

Digital Sandbox to do our last-minute preparation for the media. I remember seeing Bob Walt in the lobby . . . he was going on to another meeting. Media prep was fast-paced, lasted about an hour and helped all of us focus on key messages . . . making a real difference and driving change, empowering people, using technology and "kicking off" a revolution. Mike and Tom headed out to Bloomberg, and I had some downtime before my first interview at 9 A.M. I remember looking at my schedule, the launch plus seven different media interviews including CNN, and thinking that I needed a little break. So I took a walk on Broad Street, around to Wall Street, carrying a double espresso and my cell phone. I checked in with Kris in the office . . . everything A-OK there. On my way back to 55 Broad Street I ran into Marsden Kucera and Heidi Margulis. Knowing that we were flying out to Memphis that evening, we decided we would need to celebrate on the plane so we gave one of our drivers $80 to buy bottles of Absolut Vodka and Makers Mark for our team. Once in the Lobby of 55 Broad Street, I hung around to watch the TV monitor to see Mike on Bloomberg. He did a great job . . . and before going upstairs, I decided to get another espresso. As I was leaving the building, Diane Davis came in and said that a plane just hit the World Trade Center. My first reaction was that was really odd . . . it was a beautiful and clear day. So instead of leaving, I went back to the TV. The initial reports were confused and confusing . . . but it was becoming clear that this was a major tragedy. So I went outside to see if I could see anything, and called Alice to let her know that I was OK. I told Alice that I was fine, but that she might hear about a plane hitting the World Trade Center. In mid-sentence, I heard another explosion and watched debris come flying out of the WTC. I assumed that it was a "secondary" explosion. By this time the streets were crazed, people running, sirens blaring and a general sense of confusion. Mike and Tom made it back . . . they had seen fire and debris hit the ground outside of the American Stock Exchange. Greg Sendi and Sarah Clark-Lynn from Northlich (our PR firm) told me that my 9 o'clock interview was on hold. By about 9:15 we needed to make some decisions. I huddled with Mark Goodin first . . . then we met with David Jones and Mike. Our initial plan: cancel everything for New York, but continue with plans for Memphis. Then we heard about another plane hitting the Pentagon and other planes possibly targeting other cities. So we re-grouped and cancelled everything. At this point we were on an "execute" mode . . . figure out what we needed to do around the events, make sure that we could account for everyone, and start to think about our options. We located everyone in our group except for Bob. Steve Lieber, one of our invited guests, who was from Chicago, just happened to find his way to 55 Broad Street and joined the group. Meanwhile inside the building, people were confused. The staff did a great job to maintain calm, look for options for people to either move to the basement, or come to the fourth floor (the Digital Sandbox) where we had TV, some phones and Internet access. Among the frustrations . . . getting cell phone access. I tried calling Alice many times. At one point, I did get a message from her on my voicemail . . . she was really concerned, worried about what was happening in New York. We finally connected around 11:30 A.M. and then again around 2:30 P.M. I was able to find a land line that did allow me to connect with Kris Butler in the office to help on some of the arrangements that we needed.

My activities varied in the morning . . . from huddling with David and Mike to discuss options, to "managing" a patient—one of our team members had a panic attack—to watching TV news to keep up with what was going on. The collapse of the WTC buildings created a biblical-like event . . . daytime turned to night as the dust and debris swept down the streets. Looking out the fourth floor windows was an amazing scene. First the darkness, then the dust and silt, and then as the dust settled a scene like after a snow storm. Everything covered with a tan/gold covering, cars, the streets, and the street lamps. Truly amazing. And to think, that we just had eaten on the top of the building . . . the views, the splendor of the restaurant, and the feat of man to build something like that. Destroyed in a matter of hours. And to even think of how many victims there might be on the ground. The horror of the replays of the plane hitting the building; watching the scene of collapse over and over and thinking about our experience. And wondering if it would end. Then we heard great news . . . Bob was OK!

By early afternoon the streets became quiet. Groups had been leaving our building. David, Mike, Bruce and I huddled . . . we decided that we would gather our group up, get our belongings together and plan to leave around 2 P.M.

Several members in our group took some tablecloths, wet them and cut them into strips for masks to protect us from the dust. We were ready to go!

Like a small "military operation," we gathered everyone around the elevators and made our way to the lobby. Once in the lobby, we gathered up again, assigned "buddies" and were escorted out of the lobby through the back door. We were outside! It was smoky and dusty. Our group was dragging their luggage . . . the wheels would get stuck in the silt that covered the road. We walked east and north . . . every once in a while an emergency vehicle would pass by stirring up more dust. I remember passing by the Brooklyn Bridge and finally getting to full sunlight and a "dust-free" area.

The police directed us through a city project. In the background, we could see the smoke coming from the site of the WTC . . . again, so strange thinking about the day before and today. We were safe, in clear air, back in the world; but the world had changed. As we emerged from the project, there it was. A 28-passenger van . . . just sitting there with the hood up. Mike and I were in the lead of our group and the first to see the bus. Mike talked to the bus driver, and after a little jawboning, he agreed to take us Uptown. Initially to 25th Street . . . we hoped that he would take us as far as David's apartment. We were all pretty excited to load our luggage into the bus . . . it meant getting away . . . and it was such a surprise! Once on the bus, we started negotiating for a longer ride. The driver was on his cell phone looking for another bus that might take us home . . . to no avail. As we went further north, we convinced him to take us to Harrisburg, Pennsylvania. Why Harrisburg? David's staff in Louisville found a bus charter company that could take us from Harrisburg to Louisville. Escaping New York meant crossing the Hudson River. We did it over the GW Bridge. Again, reaching New Jersey was a real treat . . . probably the first and last time in life that I would be relieved to be in New Jersey. As we watched the WTC site fade into the distance we heard thump . . . thump . . . thump. We had a flat. Bruce was in his "territory". We got off the road in Livingston and found a few tire places . . . one had the tire we were looking for. It was about 5 P.M., time for a stretch break. Across the street from the tire store, there was a golf range . . . with sodas and snacks. I remember David paying to have the vending machine doors open so we could supply folks on the bus. After about an hour we were back on the bus . . . but trouble again. Adam the driver had a worried face . . . Bruce leans over his shoulder and says . . . "Adam are you worried about the gas gauge?" It was on "E". On vapors we got off the highway looking for a station that sold diesel. Finally, after "coasting" down a hill we found diesel fuel. The rest of the ride to Harrisburg was uneventful—I was able to call Alice a few times and found great comfort in hearing her voice and talking about what was going on, what was happening in the news and her contact with her family (including Maureen from Austria).

It was around 9 P.M. when we arrived in Harrisburg. The next scene was one of relief, confusion and negotiation. We had a beautiful big coach for the rest of the trip and we moved quickly to transfer the luggage. But we had a long negotiation between Mike, David and Adam to pay for the trip. We collected up all the cash our group had . . . were able to pay Adam and David even left him a tip. Off to dinner . . . too late for most places. We ended up at a fast-food-style sit-down restaurant outside of Harrisburg. After dinner (burgers and assorted other grease) we re-boarded the bus. Heidi brought along some Vodka . . . I had some Excedrin PM. And we had some beer. Around 11 P.M., as we rolled down the highway we distributed the "toddy" to those who wanted to sleep. Around dawn we were approaching Cincinnati and by 7 A.M. we rolled into a McDonald's in Florence, Kentucky. Again relief, we were back in Kentucky.

The last hour home . . . I remember being really tired, chatting with Mike and with a sense of relief. We were lucky . . . and we were home.

Three months later . . . how the world has changed. And how it has affected every one of our lives. But the take-home for me was a clear message—there is no control. Our fate is in the hands of God . . . and on September 11 our group was blessed.

Postscript—December 8, 2001: Visit to Ground Zero

Through a friend in Washington, Alice and I had an "official" tour of the site. Seeing the destruction in person was unbelievable. Everything from the soot, to the smell, to the sound of constant excavation were all solemn reminders of how much of the place was devastated. And the collateral damage to buildings surrounding the site—all truly beyond description. The most poignant scenes were around the different memorials that literally dot the seven-block area around and inside of the site. Seeing a newly constructed Christmas memorial, with notes from kids all around the world was yet another reminder of how blessed we are as a country.

PUBLIC
THOUGHTS
ABOUT
PRIVATE
RUMINATIONS
Heidi Margulis

I am the daughter of a Holocaust survivor . . . a fact and a heritage I cannot escape. As I gaze at our photos from *New York 9/11* and reflect on the solidarity of effort, indefatigable spirit and deep-seated compassion shown by 20+ Humana associates to each other and the cause, I am ever-mindful of other photos; *Germany 11/9* . . . 1938 . . . Kristallnacht in Mainz, Germany, when my mother, then 14, fled her burning school only to find that the Gestapo had seized my grandfather and was sending him to the concentration camp at Buchenwald. Two years, one German concentration camp, one French prison camp, two escapes and two French hideaways later, in 1941, my mother and her family disembarked at Ellis Island. Other terrorists . . . other atrocities . . . another time . . . or was it . . .

In words that have for decades resonated from teachings from the Holocaust: "Lest we forget." Lest I forget the terrible storm that kept many away from that last dinner at Windows on the World the night before. Lest I forget the sounds and reverberations from the second plane crashing into Tower 2 and my own words: "We're under terrorist attack." Lest I forget the flying debris, the suffocating smoke and ash, the darkness enveloping Lower Manhattan and the trail of Humana "buddies" with suitcases and rags over our faces walking north into the light of a beautiful day to find a way out. Lest I forget the incredible fortitude and human kindness of New Yorkers in their greatest moment of need or the fear I felt and also heard in the voices of my family. And lest I forget that while I was fortunate to get safely home in less than 24 hours, my neighbor lost her brother.

Memories on 9/11 of 11/9 were, as they always have been, perspective-setting. Lest we forget that life, no matter how good it seems at the time is never as "safe" as we think it is . . . that bad things happen to good people, not just "other" people . . . that we should never become so complacent in our own lives that we forget our responsibility to others . . . that the strength of our country lies in the diversity of our people . . . that when we stand up for our convictions, there is always a price to pay . . . the price of freedom.

It's time to move on . . . remembering . . . but laughing, caring and loving more . . . making a real difference . . . and living each day with no regrets . . . lest we forget.

Team members loading the Crystal Tours bus. From left, Tom Noland, Brian LeClaire, Bruce Goodman, Anthony Choate, Dr. Jack Lord and Mike McCallister.

THE *LINK* INTERVIEW WITH MIKE MCCALLISTER

*L*ess than an hour before the first of two jetliners crashed into New York's World Trade Center Tuesday, Humana CEO Mike McCallister started what he expected to be a full day of media interviews in New York. He and approximately two dozen other Humana associates traveled to New York to unveil Emphesys, Humana's new online insurance product.

McCallister's first interview, with Bloomberg Television, ended at approximately 8:44 A.M., one minute before American flight 11 crashed into the World Trade Center's north tower. At that point, McCallister, Tom Noland (Humana senior vice president of corporate communications) and Greg Sendi (a Humana vendor) departed the American Stock Exchange for their next destination. What follows is McCallister's account of what happened next—and then throughout the day—from his and the Humana delegation's perspective.

"By the time we got outside after the Bloomberg interview, the first plane had hit the World Trade Center. We didn't hear it hit. But we did see a blizzard of paper falling from the sky. We thought it might be a parade, although we couldn't imagine what for. We could see the Trade Center—but not the side of the building that was hit . . . We knew it wasn't a parade when we noticed some burning debris in a gutter. At that point, our driver started shouting, 'It's a bomb! There's been a bomb!' And in no time, the streets were gridlocked.

"So we decided to walk. We were just a few blocks from 55 Broad Street [location of the New York Information Technology Center]. That's where our Emphesys event was scheduled—for 10 A.M.

"And because the first World Trade Center tower had just been hit, we didn't encounter any panic on the sidewalks. We also did not yet know what had happened; we just knew something wasn't right.

"When we arrived at 55 Broad Street, we were able to watch CNN. That's when we learned about the damage to the Trade Center. We all watched the coverage in disbelief. We were very mindful that we were just five blocks away . . . And then the second plane hit. That's when we knew the first plane wasn't an accident. Of course we cancelled our event and continued monitoring the televised news coverage. I asked our team back in Louisville to send out an e-mail message from me letting everyone know that it was okay to leave work for the day.

"A little before 10 A.M., the first tower fell. The lights in our building flickered. And in just a few seconds, the world outside went dark. We were on the fourth floor [of the Information Technology Center] and could look out the windows. What was a bright, beautiful sunny day turned to black just like that. We didn't hear or even feel the tower collapsing, but it was a scary moment. We didn't know what to expect next.

"A few minutes later, building managers told all of us to go to the basement. So we did. None of us wanted to stay there though. And after just a few minutes, we were allowed to go back up to the fourth floor. Then the second building collapsed. It stayed dark outside our windows for nearly two hours—until after noon. We just continued watching it all on TV—in shock like the rest of the world. We couldn't believe all of this was happening right outside our building.

"Finally, at around 2 P.M., we decided to leave the building and start walking north, away from the scene of the tragedy. Outside our building, everything was covered with grayish-white debris. It looked like dirty snow. We each held strips of ripped-up tablecloth over our mouths as we walked through the area. We even used the 'buddy system' to make sure everyone in our group stayed together and was accounted for. Ahead of us as we walked to the north, there was nothing but blue skies. Behind us, the sky was black.

"We walked for 30 minutes or so when we came upon an empty sightseeing van. The driver was standing outside it, looking at the engine. That's when Bruce Goodman went to work. He started negotiating with this guy to get us out of New York. Somehow, Bruce persuaded him to drive us out of the city. Altogether, with the vendors who were with us, there were about 30 people in our group. And the van had room for about 30 people. It's unbelievable that we—or Bruce, rather—was able to arrange this.

"As you may know, almost every bridge in and out of Manhattan was closed by this point— around 3 P.M.—but one bridge was still open. Traffic was just creeping, but eventually, we made it to New Jersey. And the guy with the van agreed to take us all the way to Harrisburg, Pennsylvania, where the team back in Louisville had chartered a commercial bus to pick us up. We arrived back in Louisville at around 9 A.M. on Wednesday.

"The whole ordeal was something we'll never forget. But it was nothing compared to what so many other people are going through—the victims, their families and friends. We were just inconvenienced. Their lives have been torn apart. We are really very fortunate.

"I am tremendously proud to be a part of such a great company with great associates who worked together as a team during a time of considerable stress on Tuesday. And my heart goes out to all of you who've been personally affected by this national tragedy."

REFLECTIONS ON SEPTEMBER 11, 2001

Steve Moya

When we reflect on the events of September 11 our thoughts will immediately focus on the victims and their families. It will always be about them.

But being as close to the events as we were gives each of us a unique perspective that in some ways separates us from most Americans. I come away with vivid memories and a greater understanding of how as individuals we can and must look at important events from a range of perspectives.

The memories are really a series of snapshots. Walking into the lobby of 55 Broad Street and watching on television with others the "bizarre" crash of an airplane into the World Trade Center. Then, feeling and hearing a great blast with an immediate change in the area's atmosphere. Concern became fright. The next memory was on the street in front of the building where hundreds of people from the Stock Exchange were running frantically away from the destruction and what seemed like all of the paper in the world falling from the sky. Then the fourth floor where it became clear that our fates might be uncertain. Then the most powerful snapshot—the fall of the first building on television and thoughts of not only the victims, but the rescuers. Then tedium, frustration and concern until we walked out the door at two in the afternoon. As we headed home there was the view of the burning buildings from the turnpike. Finally, there was a picture in my mind of everyone in the dark trying to sleep on the bus home. It was a group that had shown great tenacity, cooperation and camaraderie.

While the memories will always be with me, so will the varied reactions and reflections on a number of different levels.

As a human being the initial reaction is to disbelieve, feel bewilderment and fear.

As a husband the desire to communicate personal safety to my wife Rita was paramount.

As a Humana employee the natural reaction was to wonder what this meant to our plans, with an immediate conclusion that it really didn't matter right now.

As a citizen of the United States there were many reactions and more questions. Why us? We didn't deserve this. How will we respond? How successful will we be? What will I be able to contribute? Will this change everything forever?

Then there is our role as members of this planet. A recent article by Francis Fukuyama brought much of my thinking about the future of the world into focus. Years ago I read his provocative "end of history" thesis. In a masterpiece of thought he concluded that the progress of mankind over the centuries toward modernity, characterized by institutions like liberal democracy and capitalism, has basically set an unalterable course for the world.

I remember thinking at the time that the conclusion seemed too neat and simple. Centuries of conflict seemed to show that the capacity for strife would always be with us and maybe even intensify. But I hoped he was right.

In the same article Fukuyama also noted a conflicting view of Samuel Harrington. I commented to someone on the bus from New York to Louisville that Harrington's book—"The Clash of Civilizations"—came to mind as we speculated on the origins of the terrorists.

Harrington argued years ago that rather than progressing toward a single global system, the world remained mired in a "clash of civilizations" where six or seven major cultural groups would coexist without converging and constitute the new fractured lines of global conflict.

These views while on polar sides represent significant insights that will play themselves out in our lifetimes. I hope for Fukuyama's world but see Harrington's as a sad possibility.

While my thought on September 11 will unfold for some time, I come away from the experience with three major lessons: know in your heart what is important and act on those things every day; while America truly values the right to be a free individual, with all that encompasses, we should always be aware of, and supportive of, the common good; and finally, we should value even small efforts to build better relations among people of the world.

One last look back before boarding the Crystal Tours bus (foreground, right) at Oliver and Madison Streets.

Photo: Diane Davis

NEW YORK, 9/11/01: 'A JOURNEY OF HORROR'

Thomas T. Noland, Jr.

The following story was published by the Louisville Courier-Journal *on September 23, 2001.*

It was one of those gorgeous, early September New York days that makes you forget what a hassle the city is—the sky arrestingly blue, the air clear, the granite and steel of the canyon-like skyscrapers at comforting right angles to the gray cement sidewalks. Those New York buildings, pushed together like redwoods in the crowded downtown financial district, bespoke power. Solidity. Stability. Permanence. The light breeze bore a hint of fall but it was plenty warm enough to walk the narrow lanes without a coat.

Humana Chief Executive Officer Mike McCallister and I entered the American Stock Exchange, just around the corner from the World Trade Center's north tower. We were beginning an exhilarating day of national media interviews around the launch of Emphesys, Humana's new Internet-based health insurance plan. Bloomberg TV had an interview booth in the Exchange. It was 8:25 A.M.

The interview rolled at 8:40 and was done at 8:45. It went well. Mike had deflected some tough questions and stayed—the PR person's mantra—"on message" about the new health plan. We left the building and walked out into the sunshine. Looking up, we both noticed the sky was filled with paper, falling in benign slow motion from, it appeared, the World Trade Center a block away. Against the bright-blue backdrop it had to be—a ticker-tape parade. Had the Yankees won the World Series again? But that would be October . . .

We got in a car and our driver navigated us toward 55 Broad Street, five blocks west, where a 10 A.M. Emphesys news conference was scheduled on the fourth floor of the New York Information Technology Center. The paper kept showering down, but we saw now that it wasn't only paper. There were chunky bits of steel falling faster; and then, in the gutter, we saw a flaming piece of debris.

"Oh my God! Oh my God!" the driver yelled. "It's a bomb! There's been a bomb! Oh my God!" People began running toward us from the trade center corner. Traffic was gridlocked.

"We're getting out," Mike said.

"No," said the driver. "You stay."

"No," Mike said. "We go."

We quickly walked the rest of the way to 55 Broad. There was a different smell to the air, an admixture of something industrial and sinister. Mike thought it was jet airplane fuel.

But how could that be?

At 55 Broad, we pushed through the revolving door and were enveloped by the crowd in the lobby, watching—not the continuous Humana videotape loop on the huge wall monitor, but a tiny TV on wheels tuned to CNN. The CNN camera was trained on the twin towers. One had smoke and flame pouring from a gash in its side.

Someone said, "An airplane just crashed into the World Trade Center."

What a dreadful accident, I thought. But inevitable. Bound to happen sooner or later. I remembered John Kennedy Jr. as emblematic of all the inexperienced private-plane pilots who could have made such an error, even in the cloudless daylight. As bad as it was, it seemed . . . manageable.

My thoughts thus turned to getting Mike upstairs to the fourth floor, where our news conference was set up, and running him through a final rehearsal. I was annoyed that he and about 10 other Humana executives essential to the presentation were riveted to the television. By now it was 9 A.M. Didn't they understand that our guests, carefully wooed and cultivated over months—key constituents, essential to our success—reporters from the Associated Press, the Wall Street Journal—would begin arriving in minutes?

And then the second plane hit.

People gasped. I went from the elevator bank to the TV and took my place in the forest of blank faces. A horrendous plume of smoke and fire breathed from the second tower, a wound beyond belief. With both buildings burning, it was clear this was no accident. Some kind of unfathomable military attack was under way—five blocks from where we stood.

"We need to go up," I said to Mike, "and get on the phones and cancel our event."

He went with me. On the fourth floor, we turned left into the side room that had served as the venue for our crisp media question-and-answer prep session 90 minutes before. Now it was filled with strangers. Each stranger's ear was attached to a telephone handset, and each set of right- or left-hand fingers was futilely punching the number buttons, trying to connect with the suddenly dangerous world outside.

"The phones are dead!" someone yelled. But the concert of fingers kept punching away. Someone found a working speakerphone in a small anteroom. Then people began getting through on a few other land line phones.

We gathered around a television in the Q and A room, and after a few minutes, the south tower began to fall. It collapsed in a sickening thud that made the lights flicker and turned outside from day to night—from clear to black—as a massive wall of dust rolled down Broad Street.

A voice came on the building's intercom and announced that we should all go to the basement. For the first time, immediate peril to our group seemed real. Was lethal dust seeping into the building? If so, why the basement? The basement was somewhere I knew I didn't want to go; it summoned images of a concentration camp—the sudden and final stopping-point in a journey of horror that had begun only minutes before.

Jason Largever, who works for the Information Technology Center, was herding us toward the elevators.

"Why do we have to go down there?" someone asked.

"It's best," Jason said.

He was doing his best to reassure us but he was doubtless as disoriented as everyone else. I'm certain he thought we might be the next building to be hit or bombed, or have another building fall on top of us; and if so, the safest place to be was underground. But it was further disconcerting when Jason said we had to leave our luggage on the fourth floor. Being without luggage took away a psychological prop, and such props were scarce right then, hundreds of miles from home with any kind of transportation a thing of the past.

We entered the freight elevator. After a short ride down, we walked into a low-ceilinged room with a few chairs and tables—very spare. Someone said, "I'll go up to the fourth floor and make a food run." There was plenty of food up there from our cancelled news event.

I took the chance to escape the basement to help with that run, and was seized with panic when I came into a hall and couldn't find any stairs. The elevators weren't working. Someone found the door to the stairs, opened it and said, "Put a shoe in this so we can get back out if we're trapped." We climbed the stairs. The door to the fourth floor was open.

Within minutes the rest of our team joined us (some hadn't gone to the basement at all, it turned out). As the dust was settling from the south tower's collapse, making it possible to vaguely discern the shapes of buildings out the window, the north tower came down. Once more the outside world went black.

We fell into a routine of watching television, making phone calls from the three or four phones that worked, munching pieces of kiwi and honeydew melon and staring through the windows, seeing nothing.

People were calm and very supportive. Every so often, the intercom voice said doctors were in the building and medical help was available. That was reassuring. After an hour or so, the second dust cloud began to settle, slowly revealing an unreal scene outside.

Cars, streetlamps, stray boxes—everything was thickly covered with dust. It looked like it had snowed gray. There was the same sense of eerie quiet that comes after a heavy snow. The streets were empty except for a couple of guys peering out from an entryway, and an occasional person walking rapidly to the north, mouth covered with cloth. No vehicles moved; the few parked cars looked like abandoned dust sculptures.

At 2 P.M., as the air became clearer, our group's thoughts turned to leaving the building and walking . . . somewhere. There was talk of an apartment on 25th Street, a block of hotel rooms someone had reserved near the United Nations and a second apartment further Uptown. In all, our group was 23 Humana associates and seven partners from the high-tech companies that had helped us create Emphesys, most of us with suitcases on wheels.

We tore up white and black tablecloths into strips, soaked them in water and tied them around our nose and mouth to keep the dust out. The "buddy system" was chosen to keep track of each other and avoid getting lost.

We left the building and started walking north. It was deathly quiet. Occasionally, a dust-covered fire or police vehicle rolled by. Ahead, despite the uncertainty of our objective, was blue sky and hope. Behind us was a moonscape of devastation, with the smoke plume from the trade center site (no one yet called it "Ground Zero") turning blacker as we went away.

After about 30 minutes, people doing ordinary things—walking their babies in strollers, eating popsicles on benches—joined the landscape. It seemed sudden to me, like the moment in "The Wizard of Oz" when black and white gives way to Technicolor. Most of us took off our tablecloth masks.

Parked by the side of the road was a Crystal Tours sightseeing bus, with a phone number on the back to call for reservations. It was empty, with the hood up; the driver, Adam, peered into the engine. Several of our group began negotiating with Adam by increments. First they persuaded him to let us on—already a stretch, to my mind. We loaded our considerable luggage in the back. Amazingly, there were just enough seats for everyone but one (who stood), along with a New York social worker who climbed aboard with us. It turned out she was a 1948 graduate of the University of Louisville.

As we rumbled Uptown, the issue of how far Adam was willing to take us was delicately vetted. First it was a few blocks. Then it was Midtown Manhattan. Then, incredibly, I saw we were headed for the George Washington Bridge. That meant escape—it was the only open artery out of town. In the opposite direction, nothing. Authorities had sealed off access to New York.

Following a flat tire in northern New Jersey, Adam drove us all the way to Harrisburg, Pa., which we reached about 9 P.M. We had arranged through our Louisville office for a chartered Trailways bus to take us home. Most of us slept fitfully until we stopped at a McDonald's in northern Kentucky about 6:30 A.M. They had newspapers there. Our group fell mostly silent. Reading about the event somehow seemed worse than having been near it.

We arrived back about 9 A.M. No one in our group was killed, no one hurt. Everyone had stayed poised, helpful and empathetic through a harrowing 24 hours. It made me proud to be part of Humana.

As with all Americans, it's been a struggle since September 11 to concentrate on the ordinary. We've taken strength from our colleagues and many others around Louisville who've expressed their support, and from the need to attend to "business at hand."

This week, for example, we're working on plans to launch Emphesys in the fall—at the New York Information Technology Center.

(Reprinted by permission from the Louisville *Courier-Journal*.)

The horrific terrorist attacks on the World Trade Center, the Pentagon and the plane crash in Pennsylvania on September 11, 2001 changed forever freedom as we have known it and in many ways have taken for granted.

I am not old enough to have lived during World War II. As the dependent of a father who spent 30 years in the military, I was in Europe during the Vietnam War and so war-related protests and other war-related events occurring in America were distant and didn't carry the impact they did for those living in the United States.

This tragedy did have impact. I was there, in New York City, staying at the Marriott World Trade Center. I was among a group from Humana who had gone to the Big Apple to promote the company's new digital health plan with a launch to the national media and tech analysts.

A half dozen of us from Humana were staying at the Marriott World Trade Center and the remainder of our group stayed at the Marriott Financial Center Hotel just down the street less than three blocks from our hotel. My boss and I had just left the Marriott World Trade Center at 8:40 A.M. when the first plane hit the north tower. We actually never heard it, nor did we see it, at first. I couldn't help but think, "If we'd left any later, I wouldn't be writing my thoughts on paper." We got out by the grace of God.

We were on our way to pick up a couple of other colleagues at the other Marriott hotel and as we were making our way up West Street, we could see some commotion ahead of us. A policeman was directing traffic away from the area. A man got out of his car and was pointing up, but we couldn't see what he was seeing. We'd connected with our colleagues by cell phone to let them know we were delayed. They had managed to get on one of the vans and thankfully, were on their way as we were to the Digital Sandbox, the site of our media launch. We said we'd meet them there.

As we drove away from the World Trade Center, that's when we saw the north tower on fire. We still didn't know what had happened. Our driver said it appeared that the area was going into a "lock-down mode" so he knew he'd only be able to get us somewhat close to the Digital Sandbox at 55 Broad Street.

As we got out of the car, we heard the second plane hit the south tower, but we couldn't see it. Then someone on the street said a plane had hit the World Trade Center.

I was thinking to myself, "That can't be right. There's not a cloud in the sky." Somehow I knew it wasn't an accident. As we walked along Broad Street, we saw a mass exodus leaving the New York Stock Exchange. Looking up in the sky, I saw bits of paper and debris floating down, almost in slow motion. The sudden realization that bits of glass also were coming down made us realize we needed to get to our destination quickly to avoid getting hit.

When we arrived at the Digital Sandbox, minutes later, and saw the replay of the second plane hitting the south tower of the World Trade Center, we realized we were under terrorist attack. I'm not sure it really sank in completely. It's as though my brain wasn't making the connection with what I'd just seen on TV. It was very surreal. After we heard a news report that the Pentagon was hit, I couldn't help but think, "What are they going to hit next? Are we sitting ducks in this building?" The feeling that there was no safe place at that moment was overwhelming. As Americans of the baby boom generation, we had never really personally experienced this type of terror in our lifetime.

My initial thought was to contact my parents so they'd know I was OK. Thankfully, they hadn't yet seen the news, so I was the first one to tell them what was happening. I kept them updated throughout the day as to what our next moves were going to be. Early on, we didn't know if we'd get out of New York City because so many other people were obviously trying to get out, too.

Later in the morning, we were ushered to the basement of the building, I went down thinking, "OK, they want everyone to be safe," as safe as we could be under the circumstances. I went down to the basement and with no windows to see the outside world, I really felt trapped and alone. I realized that none of the Humana team I was with had gone down there, or I didn't see any of them. After about 10 minutes, I took a chance and climbed the stairs to the fourth floor to find my colleagues. We were told over a loudspeaker that staying on the fourth floor was OK.

As the hours went by, I really believe we were all in survival mode but also shell-shocked as well. When the south tower fell later that morning, it is as though the world outside went dark very fast. It was very eerie and hard to fathom that a 110-story building could go down so quickly into a pile of smoke and rubble. It's still hard to believe that both towers are no longer standing. I'm not even a New Yorker, but just seeing them rising above the Manhattan skyline one day and gone the next is unreal. What's even sadder is the loss of life. I thought of the people being trapped in those buildings and wondered how many could get out safely. I can't imagine what their loved ones must be going through.

There's a saying that states that something good always comes from something bad. In this instance it may be hard to see the good. For me, the fact that all of us from Humana made it out safely, without injury and back to Louisville is just one example. As a group, we all pulled together and truly were supportive to each other.

The staff at the Digital Sandbox remained calm and collected as they provided us with access to outside phone lines for long-distance calls since most of our cell phones were no longer functioning. They hooked up a large-screen TV so we could keep abreast of what was happening. Someone brought in bottled water for everyone and they announced that a physician was available to see those who may need medical attention.

I didn't know it at the time, but a very dear friend of mine, who knew I was in New York, had emailed the ministers and staff at my church to ask for prayers on my behalf. They didn't know until the following day that we all made it back safely. Their outpouring of support has been tremendous during this time, especially since I have no family in Louisville.

The concern for our well being by co-workers back in Louisville while we were in New York City and in the days that have followed also has been remarkable. The horrific events of what began as a beautiful morning created an unknowing bond among those of us who were there as it has for the rest of the country.

As has been said in countless news reports, the caring, concern and simple human kindness in ways that are too many to count are the blessings coming out of this national tragedy.

Scene from the northeast side of Ground Zero near Madison Street.

THE END —
AND A
BEGINNING

Gene Shields

The story of our Humana team's odyssey has been told—to our friends, to our families, to the media. However, the end is not yet known. Our country has a long road to travel and the end is uncertain—will we lose more? Will we have to face the prospect of more innocent victims on both sides of the world? While in Germany more than 10 years ago, my medical staff and I supported care for the hundreds injured in the "Flugtag" air show disaster. The tragedy and horror remain with us to this day. But there is another artifact—the pride we feel about helping others in their time of need. Everyone in New York, our other associates isolated and stranded in other parts of the company, and our families will all carry disturbing memories of September 11. The hard edge of those memories will be softened by the efforts we make to care for others.

RELEARNING THE BASIC THINGS

Fred Smart

Let me tell you about the day the sky turned black in New York City. About a day when those of us who thought we could imagine anything, saw the unimaginable. A day when evil came upon us, literally, from out of the blue.

I was on my way to New York for a presentation scheduled for Tuesday, September 11, 2001 at the New York Technology Center at 55 Broad Street in Manhattan, just down the street from the New York Stock Exchange. I work for Humana, a large health insurer. Myself and six other coworkers flew out of Louisville on Sunday afternoon for Memphis, where we were to connect to a direct flight to New York LaGuardia. Our job was to get the meeting site ready for Tuesday's presentation.

We left Louisville on time at 3:45 P.M., but when we reached Memphis we found that our plane had been delayed because of bad weather that had swept through the midwest all day long and had yet to leave New York. By the time it did reach Memphis and was readied for the turnaround, it was around 8 P.M. We got into LaGuardia at 11:30. Another half-hour to get bags, it was 12:30 A.M. Another half-hour into the city, it was around 1 A.M. when we reached our hotel, the Marriott Financial Center at 85 West Street, two short blocks from the World Trade Center. That three-hour delay that left us tired and so irritated, now seems to be the most minor of travel irritation and inconvenience.

On our approach to LaGuardia, the captain told us we would be taking his favorite route to the airport, the path that takes you directly up and over the length of Manhattan. The city below sparkled from the lights of a million offices and apartments as we flew directly over the World Trade Center towers.

We didn't have much sleep that night. I was too wound up from the trip and didn't get to sleep until around 2 A.M., with a 7 A.M. wake-up call to come.

At 7 A.M., my wake-up call came and I pounded on the snooze alarm for about a half an hour. I showered and went up to the club level reception area for the free coffee and pastries. From the 38th floor of the hotel, you could see the Statue of Liberty, still standing watch over New York Harbor. I always have this great feeling when I see that landmark. I like New York and that statue, which stands at its gateway to the other side of the world, represents a sort of "welcome back" sign to me.

Stuffed with sugar and caffeine, I walked up West Street to the Marriott World Trade Center to meet Dick Brown, our Director of Media Relations, his co-worker Mary Sellers and Sarah Clark-Lynn from our public relations company, Northlich, based in Cincinnati. We had breakfast and at around 9 A.M., the four of us went out the back door of the Marriott and onto the central plaza of the World Trade Center complex. It was about 8:45 A.M., September 10, 2001.

During the day we made our plans for the next day's meeting and finished up around 6:45 P.M. I went back to my hotel, changed and took a cab to 21 Pecks Slip in South Street Seaport to meet my aunt and uncle, Madge and Bernie Rothzeid and my cousin, Alexander, for dinner at Quartino, a small Italian place located on the corner. After dinner, we walked through the shopping area of the Seaport. They took me back to my hotel, but, even though I hadn't had much steady sleep, I still wanted to get out and walk around, smoke a cigar and take in a little more of New York.

So, I went to my room, changed shoes, grabbed a smoke and went down to the street. I crossed over West Street and walked over to the esplanade of Battery Park City, a fairly new development on the western most edge of Manhattan by the Hudson River. I walked over to the edge of the park, where a marina juts into the park-like setting, lit up my cigar and just stood there, looking up at the twin towers of the World Trade Center. I can't recall what I was thinking at the time. I was just taking in the power of the city. The furthest thing from my mind was that in less than twelve hours, someone would bring the whole thing down into a pile of rubbish. I walked back to my room, ironed my shirt for the next day, watched some football and went to bed.

We had discussed on numerous occasions what time we would arrive at the New Technology Center at 55 Broad Street. Our meeting was to start at 10:00 A.M. We had invited the guests to come at 9:30 A.M. for coffee. We had the room set. Displays were up. Audio and video were ready. Materials were at hand. There was nothing left to do. So, being a little light on sleep, we asked ourselves why we couldn't wait until around 8:45 to 9 A.M. to get there. So we decided that we would meet in the lobby of the Marriott World Trade Center at 8:30 A.M. and take a van to Broad Street.

But I wanted to get up and get into the city. When I travel, I like to make a little room for local experiences, go and do where local people go and do. I like to take in the energy and the mood of different places. You don't find too many places with more energy than New York and few places in New York with more energy than Wall Street. I remember standing in room 3611, my hand on my travel bag, debating in my head if I would take off on my own or just relax with breakfast in the hotel and walk over later.

Impulsively, I decided to bag the van ride, skip the complimentary continental breakfast I had enjoyed the morning before and set out among the natives in search of espresso.

I had given some thought, as did we all, as to what to do about baggage. Originally, we thought we would check out, store our bags with the hotel and retrieve them in the afternoon after the show. But I thought that would take too much time since we had to take down the "set" from the meeting, pack it up and be at Teeterboro Airport in New Jersey to take a private jet to Memphis by 5 P.M. So I took my luggage, a small carry-on roller bag, with me.

I went down to the street and left the Marriott Financial Center behind. I had on a white French cuffed dress shirt with some cuff links that my daughter, Jennifer, had given me, a navy blue suit, an orange bow tie with tiny blue pin dots and black cap-toed dress shoes. Except for the suitcase, I fit right in with the other "suits" on Wall Street.

When I got down to West Street, I wanted to take pretty much the same route as we had taken the morning before but I thought that would be a little out of the way. The Marriott World Trade Center was north of my hotel, about a half block, but the meeting was actually east and a little south of where I was. Walking north, then walking south wasn't very efficient. But I was a little confused as to exactly how to get to Wall Street and Broad. So I walked out of the hotel, walked the short half block north then cut over to walk east on Cedar Street. But it was a dead end and that forced me up to Liberty. It was Tuesday, September 11, 2001 and I'm standing directly under World Trade Center Tower Two. It was 7:50 A.M.

I walked down Liberty, across Broadway to Nassau and turned right. I then walked down Nassau, which turns into Broad Street when it meets Wall Street at the corner of the New York Stock Exchange Building. I remember walking past the coffee vendor on the corner and watching as the traders and NYSE employees had to show their security badges to get in. Next to that door was another door marked, "New York Stock Exchange, members only."

The day before, I had scoped out a coffee shop just down the street from the exchange and just across the street from the meeting site. It was called Timothy's Coffees of the World. I ordered a triple espresso (I like espresso!) and a raspberry scone. I took a seat at the window counter, pulled out my USA Today and enjoyed being in the middle of Wall Street.

In about twenty minutes, I was done. I rolled my bag out of Timothy's and crossed Broad Street. It was 8:25 A.M.

The New York Information Technology Center is not an exceptionally impressive building, inside or outside. But it is wired to the hilt and we needed a facility where we could showcase our Internet health insurance plan with high-speed access and be located where we could get our biggest exposure to major media outlets. Our PR people had come up with the Technology Center's Digital Sandbox.

I stored my bag in a closet and joined some of the Humana people who were already there. Mike McCallister, Humana's CEO and president, was scheduled on Bloomberg Live, so we went back downstairs to watch on the large screen TV in the lobby. When the interview was over, we went back upstairs and began to wait for the others to arrive.

Soon after we reached the fourth floor, someone walked by and said, "We just got a call that a plane crashed into the World Trade Center." It was about 8:50 A.M.

My immediate thought was that this was a hoax or some kind of gross rumor. How could this be possible? But since we were set up for a demonstration of our new Internet health insurance plan, we had a number of computers at hand. We immediately pointed the browsers to cnn.com. They already had a picture.

But from the picture, it looked like a small plane, like a Cessna, or a helicopter had indeed rammed one of the Towers. A helicopter seemed more likely to me because there are helicopter shuttles to Lower Manhattan. What we failed to realize was the size of the towers and the scale of the dark and smoking wound that was apparent on the tower's face. I remember thinking, "Was anyone hurt?"

My next thought was about media coverage for our event. Any kind of coverage we would hope to get was probably going to be overshadowed by what had just happened a few blocks away.

I had no idea.

Then we heard that another plane had hit the World Trade Center. Now everything had changed. It was about 9:10 A.M.

At that point I felt like I had stepped into another world where you can't believe what is real because real can't be true. It was a state where what was happening had to be fantasy, had to be fiction because if it wasn't, then the reality was simply too unbelievable, too hard, too impossible to grasp.

Some of us picked up phones and made calls, calls to family, co-workers, and concerned friends who were now sending us information about what was happening just blocks away from us. Two planes had crashed into the World Trade Centers. Not Cessnas or helicopters but commercial airliners. Hijacked commercial airliners. Planes full of people. Now a plane had gone into the Pentagon, a fourth plane had been hijacked. People were jumping out of buildings from a thousand feet in the air.

At this point, I began to experience my first feeling of any kind of danger. Two planes had gone into the World Trade Center, a plane had gone into the Pentagon, another had been hijacked and I'm a half block from the New York Stock Exchange.

By this time, the people at the Technology Center started to hook up televisions and we watched with the rest of the world. We watched the fire and the smoke. We watched a nightmare. The media was on all of this within minutes after it happened, it seemed. Pictures of the smoking buildings were being delivered from all angles as the commentators grabbed for details, facts, explanations, theories . . . anything to come up with words to go along with the pictures we were seeing. The commentators were as dazed as we were, struggling to do anything but just stare at the images and be confused.

At 9:59 and again at 10:30 A.M., there *were* no words to match the pictures. The towers of the World Trade Center, each 110 floors and nearly a quarter of a mile high, collapsed. We watched the television, most of us with our hands to our faces, as they fell into a pile of dust, smoke, pulverized concrete and contorted steel. Thousands of people murdered right in front of me.

Outside of the conference room where we were sequestered was a small office that faced a side street. It was a bright, sunny day in New York but in seconds after the first tower fell, the sunshine was blocked by the dust that rushed down the streets like a wall of water from a broken dam. The sunlit day turned to midnight black. You could not see across the street. You couldn't see two feet away.

It was odd to watch all of this unfold on television while the reality was only a few blocks away.

It was, in some sense, filtered. I saw it not with my eyes but through the lens of a camera. But that wall of smoke. I saw that and not through a picture tube. The dust made it real for me.

When the smoke cleared, what was left was another eerie scene: a landscape covered with what looked like gray snow. Everything—cars, signs, and window ledges—was covered with a half-inch of this gray, powdery soot.

One of the things that became very real to me as time passed were the two kinds of people grouped together in our building. There was our group from Humana and other business people from out of town who just happened to be there on that day. But then there were the others, the natives, and the people who worked there. This was their neighborhood. They had friends close by, just like I have friends who work in Aegon Tower or National City or PNC. So when we watched a replay of the Trade Center collapse and I saw a young woman double over, sobbing without consolation, I realized that she very well may have just watched her friends die. Maybe one. Maybe a dozen. I'll never know.

Over the next several hours, we watched, listened and absorbed the news as it came in. We had been attacked by terrorists, by the insanely criminal, who took away thousands of lives—workers, police, firemen—buried just a few blocks away.

As we watched, we also made calls back to our homes and to our families to let them know we were OK and to get what details they had. My first call was to my wife to tell her what had happened. I asked her to quickly call my daughter at her school to let her know what had happened. I called my mother. I called my aunt in Brooklyn. I just had dinner with her the night before and I had to let her know I was OK.

After the second Trade Center tower collapsed, I decided I would call my daughter myself to tell her I was still OK but also to just connect, to hear her voice. I called the school, identified myself and said I wanted to get a message to my daughter who is a teacher. Before I could say another word, the voice on the other end told me she would go get my daughter because she would want to speak with me. She put the phone down and walked away. After about a minute, I could hear footsteps returning, then my daughter's voice, shaky and on the verge of tears. It seems as though the initial message that was delivered to her was that "your father is going to be OK," and nothing more. For over an hour she had watched the images on TV and had no idea what "going to be OK" meant. When I told her I was fine, she started crying. That's when I felt things well up in my throat and eyes as I blocked back my reaction. All I felt was love.

At around 2 P.M., we were told by the building management that we might think about getting out of the area. Throughout this whole ordeal, they had been calm, thoughtful and active, bringing in water, making doctors available, and turning a technology center into a shelter. All day long, they had strongly suggested that we stay inside that shelter. They never told anyone they couldn't leave. They just suggested that we stay.

But now they were concerned about gas leaks and felt we might want to think, literally, about our next steps.

Our plan was to walk, together, all 30 of us, north out of Lower Manhattan. David Jones, the chairman and founder of Humana, had an apartment around 61st Street, perhaps four miles away. If we could get there, we would have a haven, a base camp for the next move.

I took out my handkerchief and made a bandana. Others cut up tablecloths and made masks against the dust and dirt now hanging in the Lower Manhattan air. We gathered in the lobby. Mary, with her event binder open, took roll. We were all accounted for. We were told to choose a "buddy," someone we would look out for and who would watch out for us. No one chose me as a buddy. I picked out three people I had come with on Sunday and decided to watch out for them. I would take care of myself. So, in a pack of 30, we left the lobby, navigated the back hallways of the building and emerged onto the soot-blanketed streets of New York.

The first thing that I noticed, as we began our escape, was the quiet. No cars, no cabs, no trucks, no horns. There were sirens in the distance, but here, outside the building, was almost the quiet of a snowfall, only the snow was gray.

We made footprints in the soot and ash as we walked. Initially, we headed east, toward the river, to make sure we were clear of the wreckage. After a few blocks, we turned north and headed Uptown. The streets were not crowded. The foot traffic was light, as the building occupants began to emerge and make their way out.

As we walked, the group began to spread out. People walk in tune with their personalities: some are quick and always in a hurry. Others are more thoughtful, pensive and methodical. But cooperation among the group members slowed down those out front to allow the others to catch up.

We walked through a Lower Manhattan housing project. I don't know the name. We walked a few blocks west of the Fulton Fish Market and South Street Seaport. I was there the night before.

We headed north under the Brooklyn Bridge. I had an idea that I would cross over the bridge on foot and try to find Madge and Bernie's house. But I couldn't get past what I would do once I got there. I thought my chances of getting out of New York were better staying in the group. I later joked with Mr. Jones that I felt my chances of getting home were better if I would just stand next to him!

We made our way a few blocks more. We had walked perhaps a mile to a mile and a half when we were visited by dumb luck, good fortune, the grace of God or whatever you want to call the blessings of Providence that fall into your lap. My blessing was in the form of an empty tour bus.

We had come to an intersection where, as we had encountered several times before, the intersection was partially blocked off and we were forced to detour. This detour took us east on Madison Street. At the intersection of Madison and Oliver, a small 28-seat tour bus sat at the curb, empty, with its hood up and its driver inspecting that part of the front end. It was one of those peripheral things that I took note of and thought "small van, engine trouble." But just as the group pulled even with the van, the driver lowered the hood and began wiping his hands. With that, my awareness instantly increased. This was not an empty van having engine trouble. This was just an empty van.

At that point, Mike, who was in front of me, earned his whole annual salary in an instant. He asked the driver if he was available. The driver looked at Mike and, I'm sure, saw one guy with a suitcase looking to hire a 28-seat van. But Mike quickly explained that we had a group of people just about the right size of his van and that "I'm sure we can work something out."

The next thing I know, we had a deal with the heaven-sent bus driver and we were loading our bags into the rear cargo hold. We all loaded on and headed away. Before I stepped on, I looked back at the sky we were leaving behind. It was black with smoke.

Being one of the last ones to board the bus, I sat in the very rear, on the back row's bench seat for five. As we lurched out of the Lower East Side, negotiations were proceeding at a heavy pace up front. Can you take us to 21st Street? Can you take us to 61st Street? Can you get us out of Manhattan? To Louisville? OK, then to . . . Harrisburg, Pennsylvania?

The phone lines had been burning between our group and Louisville to develop a plan of escape ever since early in the day. We looked for hotel rooms, rental cars, anything, anywhere as long as it was headed southwest. After maybe twenty minutes on the bus, Bruce Goodman announced the plan to the group: we were on our way to Harrisburg where we would have a chartered bus waiting for us to drive us to Louisville. Bruce said our best plan is to take that bus and immediately leave for Louisville, driving through the night. He asked if everyone was "on board" with the plan. The motion carried. The bus driver had somehow been convinced, and of course compensated, to drive us all the way to Harrisburg.

As we moved uptown, life seemed more normal. The sun was out, the cars weren't covered in dust, but there were people everywhere. The subways were shut down and the city buses were packed. We made our way over to Sixth Avenue, then north to 42nd Street. Traffic was heavy as we turned west on 42nd. Times Square was crowded with pedestrians. We inched along over to 12th Avenue which turns into the Henry Hudson Parkway, then headed north for the George Washington Bridge, the only bridge, to my knowledge, that was open at that point. From the time we turned off of 42nd to the time we crossed the bridge at 165th Street, it seemed like hours went by. But as long as we were moving, no matter what speed, we were making progress and we were getting out.

We finally crossed the bridge into New Jersey. As we were merging into traffic on the bridge and picking up a little speed, I looked back at Manhattan and at the black, billowing smoke rising from its bow. The heart of city has been torn out and it was still bleeding.

As we headed south into New Jersey, we drove parallel to the island. Diane Davis continued to snap her photos on the digital camera we brought along to record what had been planned that day. As we drove along, it was quiet on the bus as we all stared at the ribbon of smoke rising from the city, each with our own thoughts about the day.

It became very apparent very quickly that our chariot was not designed for the open road. This bus, as heaven-sent as it was, had no springs and no shocks. Any solid bump was a major collision with the road.

We banged along for about an hour when a sound like a blown tire came from under the bus. That was due to a blown tire under the bus, our bus. You could hear the tread thump, thump, thump against the wheel wells. Our driver got out to survey the damage and figured with three good tires on the rear axle, we could make it up the road to a turnoff. And so we continued on.

The maneuver turned out to provide one of the more exciting moments of the trip. The turnpike is designed with two "express lanes" and an exit lane with a small concrete median separating the two. To get off at that point, we had to cross that median and another lane of traffic to get to the exit. The driver slowed down and those up front called back, "How's it look?," meaning the oncoming traffic. "Not good," we responded. At that, the driver hit the gas and bounced across the median toward the exit. Horns blared and traffic careened around us as our bus dove for the exit. We made it.

We limped along slowly, the tire tread all the while whacking at the tire well, in search of a tire store. Gas stations, of course, rarely exist anymore, having been supplanted by self-service pumps and food marts. But there still *are* tire stores and we found one in this small town of Milton, New Jersey. We all piled off of the bus, our first break since we left Manhattan, to test the store's plumbing. Firestone, however, was not ready for us and had no tire to fit the bus. So our driver left us there and set off to find the bus a new shoe. Just in case, two of our guys went along, not that the driver would even *consider* moving on without us.

Across the street from the Firestone store was a golf driving range with a shop that contained a vending machine, in other words, food. Popcorn in a bag, Cracker Jacks, pretzels and sodas. It was the first food we had consumed since we left the Digital Sandbox. It was now late in the afternoon and a long time since we had gone through the last of the kiwi and cantaloupe.

Eventually, the search party returned with repairs completed. Off we went again.

At some point later on down the road, Bruce looked at the driver's instrument panel and apparently saw something that caused him to ask the driver in his most tactful of ways, "Is that fuel gauge accurate?"

The next stop was Gillette, New Jersey in search of gas . . . more precisely . . . diesel fuel. We rolled into the first "gas station." No diesel fuel. Next stop. No fuel there either. Next stop. Ditto. Seems there's not a big call for diesel fuel in Gillette. But our next stop was on the money. We jumped off and fueled up. Gene Shields even cleaned the windshield. We posed for the only group photo of the trip. We were off again.

The last leg on the tour bus was one of the more memorable parts of the trip for me. I got a chance to spend some time with Mr. Jones, just talking and listening. In the face of enormous success, wealth and fame, I don't know that I have ever encountered a warmer, more genuine and caring person. He had moved to the very back of the bus for the rest of the trip to Harrisburg, and sitting with Anthony Coate, Luisa Charbonneau, Mary and myself, he asked us about ourselves, our jobs at Humana and our families with genuine interest. He talked about his wife, his children and his grandchildren with exceptional pride. He shared with us some philosophical observations concerning what he had learned along the way about doing your best work and working passionately at something you love to do. In these times of overinflated and obese egos grown from the accumulation of a few dollars, it was amazing to find a man who, having earned monumental success by anyone's standards, has remained so basic and warm in spite of it.

At around 9:30 P.M., we pulled into the bus station at Harrisburg, guided to a safe landing through the use of a wireless phone. Waiting for us was what seemed at the time to be a luxury liner—a large tour bus where we all had enough room to spread out, each with his/her own two seats for the ride through the night. We have a photo of Mr. Jones writing out a check to our Driver the Savior to send him on his way with proof of a good deed and a job well done tucked in his pocket. Whoever he was and wherever he is, I wish him a lifetime of good fortune.

Our next move was food. A lot of businesses closed early that day, not just in Manhattan, but all across the country. Harrisburg was no different. The first place our new driver took us had closed its kitchen. It had not, however, closed its bar. So when we re-boarded the bus, members of the team emerged with several six packs of local beer in hand. (I continue to find irony in the fact that as day moves into night, it becomes easier to find a drink and harder to find a meal.)

Our third stop found an open Eat 'N Park, a local Pennsylvania chain, escaping the insistent request of some to find a McDonald's. This was slow fast food. I enjoyed a double-decker burger, an order of fries and a chocolate milkshake topped with whipped cream. I was looking for comfort in fat, grease and sugar. I found it at the Eat 'N Park.

It is interesting how people respond to an experience such as the one we had all shared that morning and how that reaction grows through the day. Some sat without speaking, listening to others share their thoughts. Some laughed and joked their way through their concern. Some who you would think would have lots to say, didn't. But each face reflected back to the others the collective shock and fatigue that we all shared.

I had trouble sleeping on the bus. I'm not used to my bed lurching backwards and forward, and swaying from side to side. I don't think there was 10 yards of straight road along that interstate and I don't think our driver found another vehicle that he didn't think he could pass. I remember trying in vain to find a comfortable position, giving up and staring at the stars, reflecting on the day's events. I had this movie in my head of falling buildings, smoke, dust and death that I could not put on pause, stop or erase. It just kept playing on a continuous loop. It finally put me to sleep.

I remember waking once to see a sign for Wheeling, West Virginia and again as we stopped at a rest area just outside of Columbus, Ohio. As September 12th's dawn broke through, we rolled through Cincinnati, Ohio and across the bridge into Kentucky . . . home.

Our final stop was in Florence, Kentucky at McDonald's for breakfast. I rarely, rarely eat at McDonald's but Mr. Jones had enthusiastically endorsed the Number 4 breakfast: a biscuit with sausage and egg, along with a patty of some substance that resembled home fried potatoes in taste, with a cup of coffee. As he unwrapped his biscuit, he said, to no one in particular, "Man, this is living!"

I am more than a little familiar with the road to Louisville down from Cincinnati. It was a quick trip, given from where we had come. At around 9:00 A.M., we pulled into the lot where the Humana planes are housed, the group quickly scattering to their cars and speeding off to their families. I hitched a ride to the terminal and quickly did the same. It felt good to be behind the wheel, in control of my own direction and destination.

I got home, ate two pieces of pie left over from my birthday party of the past Saturday and went to bed for four hours. I found out later that some went to work. Others didn't make it in for days. Mr. Jones kept a promise to a family commitment and played 18 holes of golf. Given my level of fatigue that afternoon, spending the day in a sleepy stupor, that he played golf just astounds me. I want that kind of energy.

That was my day, its prelude and its aftermath. As the weeks go by, my prevailing thought around all of this is why I was there. Of all days and given the infrequency of my visits to New York City, why was it that I was there, just blocks away from disaster, on September 11, 2001?

I don't believe that everything happens for a reason. I don't believe that some guiding power allows innocent people to die just to teach a lesson or prove a point. I believe we give things a reason so we can bring something of value away from something that makes no sense.

I stayed at the Marriott Financial Center because the Marriott Trade Center was full. I walked right under Tower Two at 7:50 A.M. instead of 8:50 A.M. because we had randomly chosen an earlier meeting time. I was safely inside and not on the street because I had decided, at the very last instant, to leave the hotel early in search of coffee, instead of having the hotel's continental breakfast as I had done the morning before.

I am unequipped to sort this out or understand it all. All I know is that I was there and, through luck, coincidence or God's grace, I am still here to share the day and my experience with others. With a lightning bolt as a prod, I have relearned the overwhelming importance of the basic things in life, however cliched that may sound. My family, my health and the sound of my daughter's voice may be all that really matters, on this, that or any other day.

EPILOGUE

On Sunday, September 30, I returned to New York City. My wife and I had planned a vacation there for months. After much debate, we decided to go ahead with our plan which was to fly to Long Island, rent a car and drive to Southampton to visit some friends, return to Islip and take the train into Penn Station, stay in the city for four nights, then take the train up to Connecticut to visit my aunt, uncle and cousin at their home in New Milford.

We visited what has now become known as Ground Zero. We stood, mostly in silence, with the other tourists at barricades set up along Broadway and stared at the incredible wreckage and site that is now a grave for thousands of innocent fathers, mothers, siblings and friends. We followed along the route I had taken that morning, picking it up at Liberty and Broadway. We stopped at the same coffee shop where I stopped on the 11th. We even went back to the Digital Sandbox so I could shake Jason Largever's hand and thank him for his kindness and calm through a truly harrowing day.

We had a good time in New York. Despite what we had read, we found life in Manhattan to be as it always has been: rushed, crowded and efficient. We were told that the restaurants were not as crowded but the theater was certainly full on Tuesday night. New Yorkers were the same as ever: alternately kind, rude, helpful and abrupt. The natives had not fled the village.

Many tourists stayed home. That's a shame. They missed a great time: an evening at Yankee Stadium, the stores on Fifth Avenue, the Guggenheim, a walk across the Brooklyn Bridge and the gap-toothed skyline as viewed from the Promenade in Brooklyn. They missed "Proof" at the Walter Kerr Theatre, dinner at Chez Josephine and, well past midnight, dessert at the bar at Brasserie. They missed the crowd in Union Square and a 40-block walk down Madison Avenue from the Upper East Side to Midtown. Too bad.

On the Promenade, I got into a conversation with a journalist from Oslo who had come to America in search of a story. He told me that the people of Norway felt a great kinship with the people of America and that he was very frustrated, as were other foreign journalists, to not be able to get information out of American authorities. He was very kind and felt very deeply about what had happened. But he said, as we parted, that if any one good thing can come out of this it is that Americans may finally understand that they do not live in a world unto themselves, that terrorism is not something that just happens in other countries and that they need to start viewing themselves as participants in a worldwide battle against terrorism. We are all in this together.

At the airport in Louisville, we arrived in plenty of time to make it through baggage check and security. It was tighter and more intense, but there was hardly anyone there. Our flight was half full. At the security checkpoint, a little girl stood in line just ahead of us with her parents, holding her small American flag. The security agent asked for the flag, tapping its tip with her finger, testing its sharpness. She walked through the checkpoint to her supervisor and presented the tiny flag. After a brief conference, she walked back through the security gate and returned the flag to its little owner. It was an event so small but so very large. Our world and our lives have changed forever. We are now not just Americans but citizens of the world.

Crossing the George Washington Bridge—the only open exit out of New York—at about 5:30 P.M.

It is almost one month to the day that I sit here and write this account. Ironically, we (the United States) attacked Afghanistan yesterday in retaliation for the September 11th bombing and entered the second chapter of this life- and country-changing process.

My adventure to NYC began Monday, September 10th as part of the senior leadership team going to visit the World Headquarters of Ford in Detroit with a visit to my friend and colleague, Dr. Vince Kerr.

Mike McCallister, Jack Lord, Steve Moya, and Bruce Goodman presented our new "Consumer-Driven Health Plan" strategy and were warmly received. I asked Vince whether he wanted to join us on the Humana jet to NYC to participate in the launch of our new digital health plan "Emphesys" on Tuesday, September 11th. He had labor issues with UAW and could not get away. We all left and arrived in NYC around 3 P.M. and adjourned to the Marriott Hotel in the Financial District (approximately one to two blocks away from the World Trade Center).

At 7 P.M. that evening, Chuck Saunders, Bruce, Eileen Hutchison, and others walked to the World Trade Center and took the elevator up 107 stories to the Windows on the World restaurant. We met others including Karen Davis, Larry Atkins, Jim Kelly and Heidi Margulis.

We had an animated discussion with Larry, Mike, and Ken Fasola around the future of health care. At 10 P.M. I elevatored down with Chuck and Jim, not even suspecting for a minute that we had just eaten the last supper ever at the Center. Chuck and I dropped Jim off at the Marriott World Trade Center and I wondered why we hadn't stayed there, it looked much more convenient. Little did we know that hotel was also T minus 12 hours for its existence.

Chuck and I walked back to our Marriott and I went up to my room. There I looked at the schedule and saw that everyone was leaving for pre-launch preparation at 7 A.M. I debated how valuable I would be at the preparation but decided that given all the launches and presentations. I had been part of, I would be useful in peppering Mike, Jack and Bruce with questions. Little did I know that if I had decided to go with Chuck at 8:45 A.M., I too would have been showered with paper, ash, and body parts.

At 7 A.M. we all left for the "Digital Sandbox". It was a beautiful day. A day that almost made you want to live in NYC. We all arrived at 55 Broad Street, had a cup of coffee in the Starbucks and went up to the fourth floor to prepare for the 10 A.M. "Emphesys Launch." At 8 A.M. Mike left for his Bloomberg TV interview. Steve Moya and I went outside for a walk. We stood in front of the NY Stock Exchange for several minutes commenting on how good it looked since it had been recently cleaned. I wanted to walk towards the World Trade Center but Steve convinced me we should hear Mike at 8:30 A.M. and we should take a short route around the block and back into the building. We did. I did eye a great-looking pizza restaurant that was just opening but left it alone. An hour later, an avalanche of debris would come down that street and literally bury that pizza restaurant.

At 8:30 A.M. we were all watching Mike on a large flat screen TV in the lobby of 55 Broad Street and we saw the first plane hit. My immediate reaction was that it was an accident. But minutes later when the second plane hit there was an instantaneous eerie feeling that this was not an accident. Almost simultaneously with the second hit we felt a large jolt in the lobby. I thought the NY Stock Exchange had been bombed but it was the WTC explosion.

Steve, Gene Shields, Marsden Kucera myself and others were outside the front entrance looking at the mass of humanity moving and the papers coming down. All of us looked at each other and thought, well maybe we should be inside. Slowly, other members of our team (23 in total) drifted in with different stories. Dust, bodies lying in the street, people in shock, etc.

David Jones, who had been having a cup of coffee in the Starbucks next door, came in. We all watched the horror for 30 minutes before going to the fourth floor. David, Mike, Bruce, Jack, Ken, Tom, Steve and I went into a small conference room and started evaluating the situation and making calls back to Louisville. Cell phones were overloaded and useless. Landline phones were good only out of NYC. I called my wife Mitzi. She was in Yoga class and wondered why I had called to tell her "I was alright." She would find out soon enough.

Just as things were settling down, we saw a huge avalanche of dust and debris (the towers were falling down). We were watching big screen TVs and we all knew there must be many new casualties with the collapse. Most of us were in a separate room watching events unfold. Some were stunned, some were in tears, most were shocked but no one panicked.

At 1:30 P.M. David, Jack and I went downstairs to assess how and when we needed to start walking out of this war zone. It looked like nuclear winter outside. White dust everywhere. Burnt pages from the towers. No people—occasional cars kicking up dust, etc. With everyone having a "buddy" we walked out. My buddies were David and Bruce. We walked outside and with torn tablecloths as respiratory masks we made our way northward.

We went two to three blocks east past the burning rubble that had been the twin towers several hours earlier. Bruce and David led with 23 people pulling rolling bags behind. We went into some projects about seven to eight blocks up and came out on Broadway. David, Bruce, Mike and I saw a "tour bus" with its hood up and we looked at each other. Bruce and Mike started negotiating for transportation. This tour bus, which looked like it was close to being on its last legs, was the best-looking bus I had ever seen. Mike and Bruce convinced the driver to take us to Midtown then to New Jersey (where we blew a tire and came close to running out of gas), then on to Harrisburg, Pa.

At 9:30 P.M. we rolled up to the Continental Trailways bus station. Mike still didn't have a final dollar cost for the bus. We said $2,000, the driver said $150 per person or $3,500. We said great. Mike turned to me and said, I hope you have cash. I said I did and made a $2,350 contribution to our effort. Others then contributed and David, holding his one check that he thought he was going to have to use to buy vans or the tour bus, wrote it for $1,000 to the bus driver for a gratuity. We then motored to Louisville.

At 9:00 A.M. we arrived at Humana Air Corporate and a very weary 23 people made their way to their homes. Upon arriving home to Mitzi, my children Mariel Francesca and Ariana Isabel, I gave thanks to being home with my family and reflected about all those families and individuals who were not so fortunate.

Monday 9/10/2001

The plan was to fly from Louisville to New York via Atlanta on Delta. I was to arrive early afternoon, take a taxi to the Digital Sandbox and see the rehearsal and practice giving demonstrations. I left Louisville on time and arrived in Atlanta ahead of schedule. I left Atlanta on time and it looked like I was going to get to New York ahead of schedule when problems began. The pilot informed us that there were bad weather and computer problems at LaGuardia airport. We circled the Greensboro, N.C., area for about two hours with the pilot giving periodic status reports. Finally, the pilot announced that we were running low on fuel and were going to land at the Raleigh/Durham airport and would wait until LaGuardia was able to receive us.

At the Raleigh airport I could see that all flights to New York were being cancelled. The pilot assured us that we had a crew and a plane and would leave for New York when the airport opened.

We took off from Raleigh about 7:30 P.M. and arrived in New York around 9 P.M. I checked into the Marriott Financial Center Hotel around 10 P.M., tired from the travel ordeal. I had used my cell phone extensively during the day to check on the status of things in New York as well as Louisville, so it was low on charge. Since the plan on Tuesday was to do the demo then fly back to Louisville, I went to sleep without recharging the phone.

Tuesday 9/11/2001

I woke at 6:30 A.M. and got ready for the day. I had made arrangements to meet Sam Garas at 8:30 A.M. to go to the Digital Sandbox and review my part in the demonstrations. I went to breakfast around 7:30 A.M. with Marcia Jaggers and Sam. Dick Zoretic and Matt Rheinhart joined us later. I had planned to take my luggage to the Digital Sandbox, but Sam convinced me to leave it at the hotel. He said we would pick it up after the show and take a taxi to the airport. My keys and cell phone charger were in the luggage.

We set out on foot around 8:30 A.M. for 55 Broad Street. I used my cell phone to call into our daily production status meeting to be sure the systems were ready to go. Everything was A-OK. The morning was beautiful, traffic was busy and the city was awake.

We entered 55 Broad Street to see Mike McCallister on the large flat screen television in the lobby of the building. His televised Bloomberg interview went well and we checked in through building security and took the elevators to the Digital Sandbox on the fourth floor. By the time we got there, the world had changed! Someone said that an airplane had hit the World Trade Center (WTC). We went to CNN's Web site and there was a photo showing the damage made when a plane crashed into the WTC. The demo was over and it was clear we wouldn't be getting the media coverage we had worked for. Chances were no one would even show up.

People were scurrying about, some going down to the street, others trying to figure out what to do next. I was still concerned about our presentation. I wanted to be sure that the Emphesys.com site would come up and I also wanted to practice giving a demonstration. I checked with Brian LeClaire to see if Bruce Goodman had everything he needed for the presentation. Brian mentioned that there was a problem with the provider directory portion of the site. I called someone in Louisville to get the problem fixed. I talked to Jeff Wood and Tim Doss. I told them about the WTC. They helped me solve the problem with the provider directory. The WTC problem was just beginning.

Mr. Jones arrived and greeted everyone. You could tell he was saddened by the WTC event. I was walking out of the room when I heard a boom and then the building shook. It wasn't long before we learned that a second plane had hit the second WTC tower.

After the second crash, our cell phones no longer worked. All the lines were tied up. We were provided ground lines, which we used to contact people in Louisville. Some of us were milling around, others were going out to the street to see what was happening. People were leaving the Financial District buildings by the hundreds.

The sky outside turned black as the first building collapsed. This set off the fire alarms in the building. We headed down the stairs to the lobby. I ran into Marsden Kucera who had been outside. She was covered with soot and looked very shook up. She said the force of the building collapsing had pushed her down the street and she was glad she reached safety as quickly as she did. Looking outside from the lobby, all I could see was gray. It was like someone had pulled down a big curtain over the windows. The building security sized up the situation and did an excellent job in calming people down. The alarms were turned off and we were assured the building was safe. The air conditioning was turned off so it would not bring in smoke from outside. Luckily, we did not lose power or water, and had limited telephone service. It could have been much worse. Building management urged everyone to go either to the basement or back up to the fourth floor. I went to the fourth floor. A small TV was set up and we watched events unfold on the news.

I was numb. I did not really comprehend what was going on. I knew that terrorists had struck the WTC and the Pentagon, but I was treating it like an event happening somewhere else, not some place just five blocks away. I kept telling myself this was happening to someone else, that I just needed to get through it and then go back to my normal life. I knew there were thousands of people being killed and injured. I expected the death toll to climb into the tens of thousands. I was sorry for those who died and for their loved ones.

For a moment, the air was starting to clear. You could see a thin layer of dust on cars, buildings and the street. Building security said we could leave, but they discouraged it. Then the sky turned black again as the second WTC tower collapsed.

Someone on staff said they had seen body parts amongst the debris. Things were awful. It was pitch black outside. Everyone was nervous and no one knew what to do. Would our building catch on fire or be damaged? But slowly the air cleared.

Around noon the cell phones started working again, although only sporadically. There were many conversations about what we should do. Many people (who had luggage with them) changed into more casual dress. Some people ate the food intended for our show—muffins, fruit, coffee and juice. We kept watching the news.

Some time after 1 P.M. the sun was making its way down to street level. There was very little action in the streets; a few people here and there, always with either surgical masks on or cloth covering their mouth and nose. I saw only two vehicles move.

It was 2:05 P.M. when we finally decided to head out of 55 Broad Street. The sun was out but there was ash falling from the sky. Mr. Jones told us he had an apartment near Central Park. We had also contacted one of the Humana pilots who was with his sister in an apartment further north. We would head to these locations.

Before leaving the building, we tore up tablecloths to cover our faces. We met down in the lobby. Mary Sellers ran through the list to be sure that everyone was accounted for. Then we all grabbed a buddy. Mine was Sam. We were escorted out of the building by security. We used maintenance halls to reach the back door. It almost felt like we were doing undercover work.

Out in the street it was eerie. Dust covered everything like newly fallen snow. It was very quiet. We went south about half a block to Exchange Street, then headed east to Wall Street. We bumped into a few other people along the way, but not many. We continued on Wall Street until we reached Pearl Street. From there, we headed north. Our plan was to walk about four miles.

The group quickly separated. Gene Shields asked me several times to slow down the people up front, but it isn't easy to get the CEO, chairman of the board and other senior vice presidents to listen. Along the way, we took short breaks. We came upon only two vehicles—emergency types. As we walked north, the dust lessened. I remember walking by a piece of paper that was charred all around the edges. I looked back to see Marsden's face expressing the effects of the terrible calamity we were going through.

As we neared the Brooklyn Bridge, we started to see more people. Just north of the bridge the police had put up a barricade. There was only foot traffic on the bridge and there were hundreds of people crossing. We could not cross the barricade and instead headed east. After a half a block, we noticed an apartment building courtyard. We took the path into the courtyard and wound our way through it and emerged on Madison Street.

After stopping to make sure we had everyone from our group, we came upon a bus sitting beside the road. The driver had the hood up and was pouring some fluid into the engine. Bruce and Mike started asking the driver if he could take us to the apartments. Some agreement was made and we loaded our luggage on the bus and started to climb in. A lady asking directions also joined our group as we were headed close to where she wanted to go.

Bruce knows New York very well and sat behind the driver to give directions. Mr. Jones sat next to the driver to let him know where his apartment was. I sat close to the front. Several of our party wanted to be left off in spots around the city. Sam's sister lives around 54th Street. Beth Bierbower had a hotel room further north where she was staying with her husband's company, and they had bus transportation back to Pittsburgh. The lady, who was a University of Louisville graduate, wanted to be dropped off in the same area as Sam. And someone else requested another stop. We hadn't gone too far when the driver had to pull over because his temperature light had come on. Turns out he had forgotten to put the lid back on the coolant fill. Luckily, the lid had dropped in a spot in the motor compartment and he was able to find it quickly.

During the drive through the city, Bruce and others were asking the driver how far he might be willing to take us. Philadelphia was the first obvious destination, but we could not get rental cars there. Several ideas were tossed around, but the idea of chartering a bus won out. Bruce was on his cell phone trying to coordinate a plan. The group was relaxed—taking pictures and thinking of breaking into Heidi Margulis' bottle of Vodka. I am not sure when the final plan was agreed to, but the driver would take us to Harrisburg, Pa., and we would take a charter bus from there home.

Some time during the trip I realized that we had boarded the bus and let a stranger get on board without any security checks. She carried a bag large enough to contain a bomb or the driver could have been a terrorist associated with the other attacks. Humana had its chairman of the board, CEO, and several senior vice presidents on board. We were very vulnerable. We were very trusting.

After dropping people off in the city, we headed west to the Hudson River, then north to the George Washington Bridge. Traffic was bumper-to-bumper. The police had a barricade up around 14th Street. Traffic sped up again once we crossed the Hudson. I could see traffic backed up for miles to get into New York. My guess is that some of those people spent the night sitting on the New Jersey Turnpike.

It was still daylight, maybe around 6 P.M. when the bus blew a left rear tire. (Luckily this bus had two tires on each rear wheel.) We moved down the road at a slower pace. We were in the express lane and the driver had to go over a cement median to get over to the access lanes. As we crossed over the lanes, we encountered typical New Jersey drivers—flashing lights, blowing horns and a refusal to slow down. When we got off the turnpike, Bruce knew exactly where we were. He even said that there would be four gas stations at the corner. There were. However, only one of them sold tires and it did not have the kind we needed. There was a Firestone station about a block down the street, but it also did not have the kind of tire we needed. But the station's operator found another place that did. The bus driver and Steve Moya went to get the tire fixed. The rest of us milled around looking for food and drink. The station was in a lower-income area . . . a mix of small businesses and houses. Across the street was a miniature golf course. Several people in our group went to look for drinks and snacks. I was getting hungry and took a walk a block or so each way to try to find something. The only restaurant we saw was Texas Barbecue. We decided not to try it. It did not look appetizing.

It was still daylight, maybe 7 P.M. when the bus returned with a new tire. We loaded back up and headed out. We were not far down the road when Bruce asked, "Is the gauge accurate?" I looked at the gas gauge and it read empty. We passed a gas station before learning that the bus took diesel fuel which was hard to find. We entered onto the Jersey Turnpike, looking for the next exit with diesel . . . the next exit had an AMOCO sign. At the top of the ramp, a small sign said the station was .8 miles away. We drove in countryside down a winding road that seemed to go on forever. Eventually, we reached the AMOCO station, but it did not sell diesel fuel either. The attendants at the station said there was another a few miles down the road. That station did not sell diesel, but said there was another station just down the road that might. We were finally able to fill the tank at this station. Some in the group took pictures and Gene washed the window. The rest of the trip to Harrisburg was uneventful.

We arrived at Harrisburg about 9 P.M. It was dark. Bruce was still on his cell phone getting directions to the bus station. We worked our way through town, making only one wrong turn. We arrived at the bus station about 9:30 P.M. I called my girlfriend Dele for the first time. I had left a message with Gene's assistant Carla during the day asking her to call Dele to let her know I was OK. Dele said she had talked to my daughters and would call them again. My cell phone was on empty. I saved what little juice I had just in case I needed to use the phone later. I saw Mike, Mr. Jones, Bruce, Gene, Jacque Sokolov and others paying the bus driver for our trip to Harrisburg.

The charter bus was much more comfortable. Everyone had two seats each. As we had come into town, there were many restaurants open. Going out of town they had all closed. But Mike, Bruce and others had bought some beer for the group. And the driver knew of an all-night spot just up the road. We stopped there about 11 P.M. and finally had something to eat and drink. I had a Reuben sandwich and a piece of apple pie, with a Diet Coke. Dr. Lord handed out Tylenol PM for those who wanted it.

Our next stop was around 4 A.M. about 40 miles east of Columbus, Ohio, at a rest area. We dragged ourselves out of the bus to stretch and take care of nature. I had been suffering from leg cramps for hours and had tried moving about and standing to relieve the pain. But they would come back within minutes of sitting in the same position again. When I came out of the restroom, I looked up and noticed what a beautiful night it was. You could see stars very clearly. Mike walked by and I mentioned this to him. We then got into a discussion of the stars and I learned that he is a stargazer. He has a telescope he uses regularly. There was an exceptionally bright planet just below the moon that night. We thought it might be Jupiter or Neptune. I thought it was good that our CEO looked at the stars. Mr. Jones said that Jacque had said that if all travel were by bus we would make our numbers for the year. We loaded up and headed for home.

It was daylight as we entered Kentucky, a little after 6 A.M. Wednesday. We stopped at a McDonald's in Florence and bought all their newspapers. We ate and read about the attack. On the bus I counted down the miles to Louisville. We arrived at Humana Air Corporate around 9:30 A.M. Mike thanked us all for being calm and cooperative. It had been about 19 hours since we left 55 Broad Street, in a different world, in a different life.

I had to hold back tears several times as I wrote this, thinking of the human loss and tragedy. I am crying now, overcome with the suffering.

Gassing up with diesel fuel in New Jersey. Front row, left to right: Mike McCallister, Diane Davis, Marsden Kucera, Jacque Sokolov. Middle row: Tom Noland, Jack Lord, Gene Shields, Heidi Margulis, Bruce Goodman, Mary Sellers, Denise Damron, Eileen Hutchison, Luisa Charbonneau, Marcia Jaggers, David Jones, Dick Brown. Back row: Steve Moya, Fred Smart, Brian LeClaire, Bob Wittenmyer, Anthony Choate.